SCHOLASTIC

Step-by-Step
Writing Lessons
for K-1

Waneta Davidson • **Deneen Wuest** • **Deanne Camp**

New York • Toronto • London • Auckland • Sydney
Mexico City • New Delhi • Hong Kong • Buenos Aires

Teaching *Resources*

Dedication

To the phenomenal Branson Primary teachers who are using the writing mini-lessons in their classrooms; and to my wonderful, supportive husband, Gene.
–W.D.

To Scott, my wonderful husband; to Lindsi and Zachary, my beautiful children; and to the staff of Branson Primary school for being our guinea pigs.
–D.W.

To Dave, my loving husband; to Stacie and Melissa, my talented daughters; and to Jared, Grace, & Olivia, my windows into the excitement of literacy development.
–D.C.

Editor: Carol Ghiglieri
Cover designer: Maria Lilja
Cover photo: Maria Lilja
Interior designer: Kelli Thompson

ISBN-13: 978–0–545–16108–4
ISBN-10: 0–545–16108–8

1 2 3 4 5 6 7 8 9 10   40   16 15 14 13 12 11 10

Contents

Contents

Introduction

Getting started with writing instruction in the primary grades can be a daunting task. Many teachers believe meaningful writing must be delayed until students know the entire alphabet or until mastery of several basic sight words is attained. The mini-lessons we have created, however, allow teachers of K–1 students to offer exciting, research-based, child-tested instruction in the skill of writing even before students have mastered these tasks.

The structured, sequential lessons present here allow for easy presentation throughout the year. Each lesson includes a list of materials, the lesson objective, a brief introduction, instruction, modeled practice, and a teacher reflection section. Many of the lessons also incorporate a time for sharing. For many lessons we suggest one or more anchor books, but these are simply suggestions and not required. We find these books work well with the lessons, but feel free to use other books if you prefer.

You'll notice that most of the sections in each lessons are *scripted*—that is, we've provided you with the actual words we use with our students. We've included these scripts because we've found, after field testing the mini-lessons, that many teachers were unsure of what language to use to scaffold students' learning. During our field testing, one teacher told us: "I once thought I could never teach reading and writing by using someone else's script, but I soon found I loved the fact that my instructions were consistent from day to day. That way I didn't have to worry that I was saying something in a way that was impeding a child's learning." So, we share our own words here in order to help you focus your energy on students' mastery of the lesson objectives rather than struggling to find clear, student-friendly language. Please don't feel you have to adhere to the scripts slavishly. Read them over and follow them closely or simply use them to inform and inspire your own teaching.

A Word About Partnerships

Many of the lessons ask students to turn to a partner for discussion or sharing. For the sake of ease and consistency, you may wish to form stable partnerships—for several weeks or longer—so that students can develop a familiarity with their partner and so that choosing a new one doesn't become a time-consuming affair. You may then want to ask students to sit with their partner whenever they come to Writer's Workshop, so they can immediately turn to their partner when you ask them to, and get right to work.

A Final Word to You, the Classroom Teacher

These lessons have been developed to offer you a guide for conducting writing mini-lessons in your classroom. In some cases, there may be too much material offered. You are best able to gauge the needs of your classroom and adapt the lessons to meet those needs. Some lessons may need to be eliminated altogether if children have already received a firm foundation from previous instruction. The lessons are paced to be used throughout the entire year, but you'll want to progress at a rate dependent upon the needs of your particular students. All classes will not progress at the same speed. Finally, these lessons are appropriate for both kindergarten and first-grade children, with first-grade teachers expanding on the materials presented and leading children into deeper discussions. We hope these mini-lessons will get your Writer's Workshop up and running on the very first day and carry you through a productive, successful year!

UNIT 1: BASIC ROUTINES

The mini-lessons in Unit 1 are designed to help you introduce some very basic routines that will facilitate listening and learning among your students, and keep your Writer's Workshop running smoothly all year long. We start you off with management basics to help build good listening habits and foster respect in the classroom. In this unit and the next one, you'll be establishing procedures and setting the stage for a productive year. Students will learn your behavior expectations, how to work with partners, and how to care for their supplies. You may wish to repeat some of these lessons as needed, to ensure children are familiar and comfortable with your Writer's Workshop routines. As with all the lessons in this book, we provide sample scripted dialogue, which we hope you'll find useful. But don't feel you have to "follow the script" verbatim in order to carry out the lessons. Use the sample language to the extent that you find it helpful.

Mini-Lesson 1:
Sitting for Writer's Workshop

Materials:
   * Writer's Workshop expectations chart   * Chart marker

Objective:

To have children come quickly and quietly to Writer's Workshop, ready to learn

Introduction:

Explain what you want children to learn today: how to come together for Writer's Workshop.

> Today I will teach you how to sit when we meet together as a group, and you will learn how to come quickly and quietly to our meeting place, how to find your spot, and how to sit quietly like good listeners, ready to learn about writing.

Instruction:

Explicitly tell children how to prepare for Writer's Workshop.

> When I ask you to join me for Writer's Workshop, please quietly stand up and push your chairs in, walk to our meeting place without talking or bothering anything or anyone, look to see that you are in the right spot, then sit on the floor with your legs in an X and your hands in your laps. Be sure you are not touching the

children next to you. Sit quietly in a good listening position—eyes watching, ears listening, mouth closed and quiet, hands and body still, and your brain ready to learn. By doing these things, you will show that you know how to be a good listener and we will have time for me to teach and for you to learn.

Practice:

Have children practice coming to the meeting place and sitting down. Call them to you one at a time and direct each child to sit in the spot you have predetermined for him or her. (Remember, you will need to have predetermined partnerships for the next day's lesson, and be sure to seat the partners together.) Act out the process until children are walking quietly to their spots and sitting down as described.

Connection:

Remind children of your expectations.

> ■ I will expect that each and every day we meet for Writer's Workshop, you will come quickly and quietly to our meeting place and you will sit down in a good listening position, ready to learn.

Create a classroom expectations chart for the Writer's Workshop, and write: "We walk quickly and quietly to our meeting place" and "We sit quietly in our spots."

Reflection:

Consider this mini-lesson. What worked and what didn't? What would you do differently next year?

_____

_____

_____

_____

How We Act During Writer's Workshop

1. We walk quickly and quietly to our meeting place.

2. We sit quietly in our spots.

Mini-Lesson 2:
Creating Partnerships

Materials:
* List of predetermined partnerships
* Writer's Workshop expectations chart
* Chart marker

Objective:

To teach children how to work with a partner

Introduction:

Explain what you want children to learn today: how to work with a partner.

> The last time we met, you learned how to sit when we meet together for Writer's Workshop. You learned how to walk quickly and quietly to our meeting place, how to find your spot on the floor, and how to sit quietly in a listening position with your legs in an X and your hands in your lap, ready to learn about writing. Today I will teach you how to work with one of your classmates who will be your partner.

Instruction:

Explicitly tell children how to work with a partner for Writer's Workshop.

> Each day when I ask you to join me for Writer's Workshop, you will walk quickly and quietly to your spot in our meeting place. You will sit down on the floor in a good listening position with your legs in an X and your hands in your lap, ready to learn. The person sitting beside you will be your partner. Most of you are sitting by two people, so I will tell you who your partner is. Listen carefully, and remember your partner's name and what your partner looks like. Sometimes when we are meeting together, I will ask you to turn to your partner and discuss something. When you turn to your partner, you will face your partner and sit knee to knee. You will then quietly talk to your partner about what I have asked you to talk about. You will look at your partner when he/she is talking and you will listen carefully. You will take turns talking and listening.

Practice:

Have children practice turning to their partners, sitting knee to knee.

> We are going to practice working with our partner. When I say, "Turn to your partner," turn to face your partner and sit knee to knee. Look at your partner. When I clap my hands twice and hold a hand up, turn back to face me and look at me. Let's practice, so you will know how to turn to your partner.
>
> (Practice until children are doing this smoothly.)
>
> Now turn to your partner and tell him or her your name and one thing you like to do. You will take turns and you will listen carefully to what your partner has to say, not talking while he or she is talking. When you hear my signal—clap, clap, hand up—you will quickly finish your sentence, then turn back to look at me, sitting quietly in your good listening position.

Connection:

Remind children of your expectations.

> I will expect that each and every day that we meet for Writer's Workshop you will come quickly and quietly to our meeting place and you will sit down in a good listening position, ready to learn. I will expect you to turn to your partner when I ask

you to and to talk about what I have asked you to discuss. I will also expect you to listen to what your partner has to say and then quietly turn back to face me when I give the signal.

On your classroom expectations chart, review: "We walk quickly and quietly to our meeting place" and "We sit quietly in our spots." Then add, "We listen to our partners when we share."

Reflection:

Consider this mini-lesson. What worked and what didn't? What would you do differently next year?

_____

_____

_____

_____

> ### How We Act During Writer's Workshop
>
> **1.** We walk quickly and quietly to our meeting place.
>
> **2.** We sit quietly in our spots.
>
> **3.** We listen to our partners when we share.

Mini-Lesson 3:
Using and Caring for Supplies: Pencils and Crayons

Materials:
* Book that models using school supplies appropriately, such as *Harold and the Purple Crayon*, by Crockett Johnson, or *My Crayons Talk*, by Patricia Hubbard
* Writer's Workshop expectations chart
* Marker
* Pencils and crayons

Objective:

To show children how to care for pencils and crayons

Introduction:

Explain to children what you want the them to learn today: how to use pencils and crayons correctly.

> You have learned how to come to our meeting place quietly and how to sit quietly beside your partner so you can learn. Today I am going to teach you how to the use the pencils and crayons in our classroom.

Instruction:

Explicitly tell children how to use and take care of the pencils and crayons in the classroom.

> ■ Pencils and crayons are a lot of fun to use, and you can create
> many wonderful drawings using your imagination. In the book
> *Harold and the Purple Crayon,* by Crockett Johnson, a little
> boy named Harold uses his imagination and makes all kinds of
> wonderful things with just his purple crayon. Listen to his story.
>
> (Read *Harold and the Purple Crayon.*)
>
> I'm sure Harold took very good care of his purple crayon because
> it was very important to him. You will find new pencils and crayons
> at your work place for you to use today and every day. I want you
> to take care of these pencils and crayons so they will last a long
> time and allow you to make many wonderful drawings.

Practice:

Have children think of ways to treat their pencils and crayons so they stay in good condition.

> ■ I wonder what you could do to keep your pencils and crayons
> so they will last a long time. When I say, "Turn to your partner,"
> turn to face your partner and sit knee to knee. Look at your
> partner and tell him or her one thing you could do to keep your
> pencils nice. When I clap my hands twice and hold a hand up,
> turn back to face me and look at me.

Give children a couple of minutes to discuss, and then signal them to stop and listen. Call on two or three children to tell what their partners said. Then add any other suggestions you would like to make.

> ■ I will also expect you to remember to take only one pencil or
> crayon out of the art supply container at a time. You will put
> it back in the container before taking another one out. That
> will help to keep your supplies from getting lost. I will expect
> you to remember never to put your pencils or crayons in your
> mouth. You are not to chew on the pencils or crayons. That
> will ruin them, and they could make you sick. We don't want
> either to happen!

Connection:

Remind children of your expectation.

> ■ I will expect that each and every day you will use your pencils
> and crayons with care. If you should happen to find a crayon out
> of place, such as on the floor, then take that crayon to this box for
> lost-and-found crayons.
>
> (Show box and where it is kept.)
>
> If you should ever discover that you have lost a crayon, you may go to
> this box to take a crayon to replace the one you have lost.
>
> If you ever find a pencil out of place, then take that pencil
> to one of these containers for pencils. If the pencil is sharp,
> put it in this container marked "Sharpened Pencils." If the
> pencil needs to be sharpened, put it in this container marked
> "Unsharpened Pencils."
>
> (Show both containers and where they are kept.)

If you discover that you have lost a pencil, you may go to the "Sharpened Pencils" tub and take a pencil to replace the one you have lost. Remember, only take one to replace the one you have lost. Never take more. That way we will always have enough in case someone needs one.

You do not have to ask me or another adult to take care of lost pencils and crayons. This is something you can take care of yourself, because now you know how to do it.

On your classroom expectations chart, review: "We walk quickly and quietly to our meeting place," "We sit quietly in our spots," and "We listen to our partners when we share." Then add, "We take care of our pencils and crayons."

Reflection:

Consider this mini-lesson. What worked and what didn't? What would you do differently next year?

_____

_____

_____

_____

Mini-Lesson 4:
Watching the Teacher

Materials:
* Books that model listening skills, such as *Look! Look! Look!*, by Nancy Elizabeth Wallace, or *Communication*, by Aliki
* Classroom expectations chart
* Chart paper
* Chart marker

Objective:
To watch and listen to the teacher

Introduction:
Explain what you want children to learn today: how to watch and listen to the teacher.

■ You have learned how to come to our meeting place quickly and quietly and how to sit quietly beside your partner so you can learn. You have also learned how to the use pencils and crayons in our classroom. Today I am going to teach you how to watch and listen to me while I am teaching you.

Instruction:

Explicitly tell children how to watch and listen during instruction time.

> Now that you are sitting quietly beside your partner in your spot with your legs in an X and your hands in your lap, I am going to share with you a book by Nancy Elizabeth Wallace. It is called *Look! Look! Look!* and it is going to remind us how important it is to look carefully so we can learn.
>
> (Read selected book to children. For this lesson, we use *Look! Look! Look!*)
>
> The mouse family in this book learned that if they looked very carefully at a picture, they could learn a great deal, and that what they learned would help them make their very own pictures. In just this way, you are going to learn that it is very important for you to watch carefully during our Writer's Workshop so that you can learn and use what you have learned to do your own work.
>
> Today and every day that you are at Writer's Workshop and are sitting in your spot, I will expect you to watch me and the things I am showing you. I will expect you to look carefully because I know that if you look carefully you will learn just as the mice did.
>
> Point to the part of your body that you look with. That's right. You look with your eyes. If you watch carefully with your eyes, you will learn. To help you watch carefully with your eyes, though, you need to make sure the rest of your body is helping you. Think how your body needs to be so your eyes can see and you can watch.

Practice:

Have children think of ways their bodies can help them watch with their eyes.

> I wonder if you could watch me or look at the things I show you if you were lying down on the floor. No, you couldn't. To watch me carefully you have to be sitting up. What else can your body do to help you watch carefully?
>
> When I ask you to turn to your partner, tell your partner one thing your body can do to help you watch me and look at the things I show you.

Allow time for discussion and sharing. Then talk about suggestions. Among the ideas suggested might be sitting with legs in an X, keeping hands in laps, keeping mouths quiet, keeping bodies still without moving around, and listening with ears. Create a chart called "Look and Listen to Learn."

Connection:

Remind children of your expectations.

> I expect that each and every day you will watch me during Writer's Workshop and look at the things I am showing you so

Look and Listen to Learn

1. Our bodies are still, and we sit with our legs in an X and our hands in our laps.

2. Our eyes look at the person who is talking.

3. Our ears listen to what the person is saying.

4. Our mouths are closed and quiet.

5. Our brain is thinking about what the person is saying or showing us.

you can learn. I would like you to practice being good watchers as we look at our chart and add what we discussed today.

Review your classroom expectations chart, and then add "We watch our teacher and what she is showing us."

Reflection:

Consider this mini-lesson. What worked and what didn't? What would you do differently next year?

_____

_____

_____

_____

> ### How We Act During Writer's Workshop
>
> **1.** We walk quickly and quietly to our meeting place.
>
> **2.** We sit quietly in our spots.
>
> **3.** We listen to our partners when we share.
>
> **4.** We take care of our pencils and crayons.
>
> **5.** We watch our teacher and what she is showing us.

Mini-Lesson 5:
Listening to the Teacher

Materials:
- Books that model listening skills such as *Listen and Learn*, by Cheri Meiners, or *Can You See What I See?*, by Walter Wick
- Writer's Workshop expectations chart
- Look and Listen to Learn chart
- Marker

Objective:
To show children how to listen to the teacher

Introduction:
Explain that today you want children to learn how to listen to the teacher.

> You have learned how to come to our meeting place quickly and quietly and you have learned how to sit quietly beside your partner so you can learn. The last time we met we talked about how to watch me while I am teaching you. Today I am going to teach you how to listen to me when I am teaching, even when other things or people may be bothering you.

Instruction:
Explicitly tell children how to listen during instruction time even when there may be outside distractions.

■ Now that you are sitting quietly beside your partner in your spot with your legs in an X and your hands in your lap, we are going to first look at the chart you helped create last time we met.

(Discuss the five points on the Look and Listen to Learn chart.)

We decided that these things are important to help us learn. I want you to remember to do these things as I share a special book with you that will help us learn how important it is to listen even when other things may be bothering us.

(Read the book you've selected. For this lesson, we use *Listen and Learn*.)

In this book, the little boy really watches and listens to his teacher even though there are many other things that might bother him.

If I am reading or writing or talking and we are here in our meeting place, how should you be sitting? Where should your eyes be looking? What should your ears be doing? Where should your hands be? What should your mouth be doing? If your body, hands, feet, and voices are quiet and still, then you will be able to watch and listen and learn.

But what if your partner isn't sitting quietly and whispers to you? Or what if your partner bumps you? Or what if a visitor walks into the room? Even though these kinds of things might happen, you should still watch me with your eyes and notice the things I am showing you, and you, should listen to me with your ears.

Practice:

Have children practice listening and watching carefully as you add to the classroom expectations chart.

■ Today and every day I want you to watch and listen when I am teaching you. We are going to practice being good watchers and listeners even if something or someone is bothering us.

(Practice different scenarios with children and allow some role-play time.)

So, when we are supposed to be listening, we need to follow the rules on our Look and Listen to Learn chart, even if someone or something is bothering us.

Connection:

Remind children of your expectations for listening.

■ I expect that each and every day you will watch and listen to me when I am teaching you, even if someone or something bothers you. When you use your eyes to look and your ears to listen, you learn new things.

Review your Writer's Workshop expectations chart, then add "We listen when the teacher is talking to us."

How We Act During Writer's Workshop

1. We walk quickly and quietly to our meeting place.

2. We sit quietly in our spots.

3. We listen to our partners when we share.

4. We take care of our pencils and crayons.

5. We watch our teacher and what she is showing us.

6. We listen when the teacher is talking to us.

Reflection:

Consider this mini-lesson. What worked and what didn't? What would you do differently next year?

_____

_____

_____

_____

Mini-Lesson 6:
Helping Everyone Learn

Materials:
* Book about group sharing, such as *Can I Help?*, by Marilyn Janovitz
* Writer's Workshop expectations chart
* Look and Listen to Learn chart
* Chart paper for Morning Message
* Chart marker

Can I Help?
by Marilyn Janovitz

Objective:

To teach children to raise hands quietly when they want to share

Introduction:

Explain what you want children to learn today: how to raise hands quietly when they wish to share.

> You have learned a lot about how to act during Writer's Workshop. You have learned how to come to our meeting place quickly and quietly and you have learned how to sit quietly beside your partner so you can learn. You have learned how to use pencils and crayons. You have also learned how to watch and listen to me while I am teaching you, even though other things or people may be bothering you. Today, I am going to teach you how you can help me and how you can help all of your friends learn when we are meeting together the way we do for Writer's Workshop.

Instruction:

Explicitly tell children how to raise their hands and wait to be called on to share.

> Now that you are sitting quietly beside your partner in your spot with your legs in an X and your hands in your lap, I would like to share with you a book that will remind us how to help in our classroom. It is written by Marilyn Janovitz and it is called, *Can I Help?*

Look and Listen to Learn

1. Our bodies are still, and we sit with our legs in an X and our hands in our laps.

2. Our eyes look at the person who is talking.

3. Our ears listen to what the person is saying.

4. Our mouths are closed and quiet.

5. Our brain is thinking about what the person is saying or showing us.

(Read whichever book you've selected.)

In this book, Little Wolf really wants to help his dad. He causes a lot of problems for his dad, but he really does want to help. He just needs to know how to help in the right way. Just like Little Wolf, you need to know how you can help during Writer's Workshop.

One way you can help me to teach and all of your friends to learn is to do what we have written on our Look and Listen to Learn chart.

(Review chart.)

Another way you can help when you know the answer to a question or would like to share what your partner has said when we discuss things is to raise your hand to share. This is very important. Instead of shouting out an answer or trying to talk louder than anyone else, just raise your hand quietly when you have an answer.

I may not be able to call on everyone every time because we have a lot of friends with answers. But when I see you with your hand raised, I will know that you have an answer and that I can call on you for help. But remember, since we do have so many friends here, we need to take turns. If I can't call on you because it is your friend's turn, does it help for you to wave your hand or shout? No, it doesn't. We need to all help in a good way and raise our hands nicely. If you're not picked for an answer this time, maybe you will be picked next time. The important thing is that we all raise our hands nicely and quietly and that we listen to our friends when they are chosen to answer. Remember, helping is very important, but always be sure you are helping in the right way.

Practice:

Have children practice raising their hands as you ask them questions.

> I will expect that today and every day you will be a good helper during Writer's Workshop by raising your hand quietly if you know an answer.

For additional practice, introduce Morning Message, if you haven't already. Each morning as you write the message, ask some questions, and have children raise their hands to be called on to answer.

> I am going to write a short letter to you. This will be my "Morning Message." I will write a Morning Message to you each and every day from now on this school year. I would like to have you help me write my Morning Message.

> I will ask you questions as I write, and if you know the answer I would like you to quietly raise your hand. If I call on someone else, you will quietly put your hand down and try to help the next time.

> (Write the Morning Message with the children's help.)

Morning Message

Dear Class,

Today is Tuesday, September 2. You have learned how to be good listeners and helpers.

Love,
Your Teacher

Connection:

Remind children how to help by raising their hands.

> Today and every day when I need your help, quietly raise your hand and then help me when I call your name. If I ask someone else to help, quietly put your hand down and try to help at another time.

Review your Writer's Workshop expectations chart, and then add "We raise our hands to give an answer."

Post the classroom expectations chart in the classroom where the children are able to see and refer to it during the year.

Reflection:

Consider this mini-lesson. What worked and what didn't? What would you do differently next year?

_____

_____

_____

_____

_____

How We Act During Writer's Workshop

1. We walk quickly and quietly to our meeting place.

2. We sit quietly in our spots.

3. We listen to our partners when we share.

4. We take care of our pencils and crayons.

5. We watch our teacher and what she is showing us.

6. We listen when the teacher is talking to us.

7. We raise our hands to give an answer.

Have children adjusted to the basic routines for Writer's Workshop? It is very important to the success of your writing program that these routines are established. If they are not, you may want to revisit this unit or approach the next unit slowly, concentrating on establishing class routines. What can you do to help ensure your students' writing success?

Unit 2: Getting Started

The mini-lessons in Unit 2 will help children get ready to write. Review the classroom expectations chart as needed as you carry out the lessons that follow. Some of what you'll find in this unit are lessons that introduce students to the writing folder, teach them what to do when they're "finished," show them how to add the date to their papers, and help them deal with distracting neighbors when they're trying to work! As with all the mini-lessons in this book, feel free to repeat any lessons in this unit for added practice and reinforcement.

Mini-Lesson 7:
Using the Writing Folder to Store Finished and Unfinished Work

Materials:
* Student writing folders, with pockets labeled "Finished" and "Not Finished"
* Your own writing, some finished, some not

Objective:
To show students how to separate finished and unfinished work in their folders

Introduction:
Tell students that they will learn where to keep their writing at the end of Writer's Workshop.

> Today I'm going to teach you how to take care of your writing. Sometimes you will want to save a piece to work on later. And sometimes you will want to store a piece that is already finished.

Instruction:
Give each student a writing folder with his or her name on it, and show them how to take care of and store their work. Tell them they will separate and store their writing as either "finished" or "not finished."

> You will see that your writing folders have two pockets inside. You will see that one pocket says "Not Finished" and the other pocket says "Finished." We can use this folder to put our writing papers in. At the end of Writer's Workshop, if you

are finished with your paper and don't have anything else to add to your picture or any more words to write, then you will put the paper in the "Finished" pocket. You will put it in carefully so it does not get bent or wrinkled. If you are not finished when Writer's Workshop ends, you will put the paper in the "Not Finished" pocket so you can work on it next time.

(Demonstrate several times with your own finished and unfinished work.)

Practice:

Give each child a sheet of paper and have children practice putting the paper into the folder pockets.

- Pretend that you have been writing and you have finished your piece. What do you do with your paper? Show me how you will put it into your folder. What pocket did you put your finished paper in?

- Now, pretend that you have been writing and you hear me say to stop and put your work away. What do you do with your paper that you are not finished with? Show me what you do. What pocket of the folder do you put your unfinished paper in?

Connection:

Tell students that each day at the end of Writer's Workshop they will store their work in their folders.

- At the end of every writing time, you need to decide where you want to put your piece. If it's finished in will go in the "Finished" pocket. If you want to add words or pictures, it will go in the "Not Finished" pocket.

Reflection:

Consider this mini-lesson. What worked and what didn't? What would you do differently next year?

_____

_____

_____

_____

Mini-Lesson 8:
Thinking Like an Author

Materials:
* Writer's Workshop expectations chart
* Autobiographies, such as *Nana Upstairs & Nana Downstairs*, by Tomie dePaola, or *Thunder Cake*, by Patricia Polacco

* Chart paper
* Marker

Objective:
To encourage children to think before they write

Introduction:
Explain that today you want children to think about what they are going to write and that they can write about experiences from their own lives.

Review the Writer's Workshop expectations chart and remind children of everything they've learned so far.

> Today I am going to teach you that authors always think before they write, and that they write about things they know about. They write about things they have done or things that they know from their own lives.

Instruction:
Talk to children about thinking before they begin. Explain that the story idea needs to be in place first, and then they can draw and write. (Many children will simply draw pictures if they are not encouraged to think of a story idea first.)

> Boys and girls, the last time we met I told you that when an author wants to write a story the first thing the author must do is to think of a story he or she would like to write. Then the author draws and writes about that story idea. Today I am going to teach you how to think of an idea to draw and write about.
>
> Authors think of things they know about. In his book *Nana Upstairs & Nana Downstairs*, Tomie dePaola wrote about his two grandmothers. In her book *Thunder Cake*, Patricia Polacco wrote about how her grandmother taught her that she was a brave girl, even though Patricia thought she was afraid of almost everything. In the story I wrote last time, I told about something that really happened to me. So, authors think of things they know about. Then they write about those things.
>
> (Model thinking of something you know about, then writing about it.)
>
> Today I am going to write a story. Let's see. I could just draw a picture of pretty flowers. I like flowers. But, would that be something that happened to me, something I really know about?

I know—I'll think first!

> (For fun, exaggerate your thinking—finger to forehead, frowning, eyes looking up.)

I have it. I'll write about _____.

> (Sketch your idea while talking about it.)

Now I have my sketch, my really fast picture. Now I will write my words.

> (Under the picture, write your story, saying the words slowly and matching the word you say to the words you write.)

Practice:

Have children think of a story idea, then turn to their partners to share.

> ■ Boys and girls, think of something you could write about today. Think of something you have done or something from your life. Now, when I ask you to, turn knee to knee to your partner and tell your partner what your story idea is. Remember to take turns with your partner.
>
> > (Allow a few minutes, and then give the signal for children to stop and face you.)
>
> I heard several good ideas for stories. I am excited to see your work.

Connection:

Remind children to write about their own lives and remind them how to use the writing folders.

Dismiss children from the group a few at a time and comment on the things you see them doing right as they go back to their seats. You may also use this type of dialogue to lead those children who are more reluctant to begin.

While children are working, conference with them, especially with those who are unsure about how to begin.

Reflection:

Consider this mini-lesson. What worked and what didn't? What would you do differently next year?

_____

_____

_____

_____

Mini-Lesson 9:
When You're Finished...

Materials:
* Writer's Workshop expectations chart or the Look and Listen to Learn chart
* Books by Tomie dePaola and Patricia Polacco
* Two sheets of chart paper to model your own writing (one writing almost finished)
* Marker

Objective:
To help children continue writing during Writer's Workshop

Introduction:
Explain when children "finish" a piece during Writer's Workshop, they should not stop working. They may wish to add on to the piece or start something new.

Review the Writer's Workshop expectations chart or the Look and Listen to Learn chart. Use these charts to keep the classroom standards of behavior in children's minds until they internalize them (which for some may never happen!).

> We know that authors always think before they write and that they write about things they have done or things they know from their own lives. But many authors say, "When you are done, you've just begun." What does that mean? When Tomie dePaola finished *Nana Upstairs & Nana Downstairs*, he started another book. When Patricia Polacco finished *Thunder Cake*, she started another book.
>
> (Hold up a few books the authors have written.)
>
> Just like these authors, when you finish a story, you can start another one. But before you do that, you may want to add more to the words of your first story, or you may want to add more to your picture.

Instruction:
Explain to children that Writer's Workshop is a time that's dedicated to writing. When they finish a piece, they should continue working on that piece of writing or start a new one.

> Boys and girls, I have a story here that is almost finished. Watch as I finish my last sentence.
>
> (Finish your first story.)
>
> There, I'm done!
>
> But, wait! Authors say, "When you're done, you've just begun." I've just begun. What should I do? I know. I can add to my picture.
>
> (Add some details to the picture.)
>
> I can also add to my words.
>
> (Reread what you have written, and then add to the words.)

▪ Or, I can start a new piece of writing.

(Get out another sheet of paper and overexaggerate thinking. Then start a drawing.)

Wow, authors are right. "When you're done, you've just begun." I can add to my picture. I can add to my words. Or I can start a new piece of writing.

What Do I Do When I Finish a Piece of Writing?

1. I can add to my picture.

2. I can add to my words.

3. I can start a new piece of writing.

Practice:

Have children work with you to make a chart of what to do when they have finished a story. Ask then to offer their ideas, which should include the ones you've taught.

▪ Boys and girls, help me make a chart of what to do when you have finished a piece of writing.

Work together to construct a chart that you can post in the classroom.

Connection:

Remind children to write from their lives and to continue working when they finish a piece of writing. Also remind them how to use the writing folders.

▪ I know that today you will think about what you are writing and that you will write a story from your lives. I know that you will remember what to do when you finish a piece of writing. I also expect you to know how to take care of your writing papers during Writer's Workshop and that you will stop working when I ask and you will put your paper in the finished side if you are done with it, and the unfinished side if you have not yet finished.

Dismiss children from the group a few at a time and comment on the things you see them doing correctly as they go back to their seats. You may also use this type of dialogue to lead those children who are more reluctant to begin.

While children are working, conference with them, especially with those who are unsure about how to begin.

Reflection:

Consider this mini-lesson. What worked and what didn't? What would you do differently next year?

_____

_____

_____

_____

_____

Mini-Lesson 10:
Working With a Partner

Materials:

* Book that illustrates how to work well with others, such as *Cowgirl Kate and Cocoa*, by Erica Silverman
* Chart paper
* Marker

Objective:

To teach children to work successfully with a partner

Introduction:

Explain that today you want children to focus on working well with a partner.

> You have learned how to sit beside your partner and how to turn to your partner knee to knee, and how to take turns talking. Today I am going to teach you other ways your writing partner can help you.

Instruction:

Explicitly tell children how to work with a partner for Writer's Workshop.

> Boys and girls, when you join me for Writer's Workshop each day, you sit quietly beside your partner. Sometimes I ask you to turn to your partner and discuss something. When you turn to your partner, you face your partner, knee to knee. You then quietly talk about what I have asked you to discuss. You look at your partner when he or she is talking and you listen carefully. You take turns talking and listening.

> It is very helpful to have a partner. I would like you to listen to a book called *Cowgirl Kate and Cocoa*, by Erica Silverman. It is a chapter book, so we're just going to read a little bit right now. I'd like you to listen to see how Cowgirl Kate and Cocoa help one another.

> (Read a chapter of this book, or another book you've chosen.)

Practice:

Have children turn to their partners, sitting knee to knee, and discuss the story.

> Boys and girls, think about how Cowgirl Kate and Cocoa helped each other in the story we read. What is one way they helped one another? Turn to your partner and talk about it.

Signal for children to finish talking and sit quietly for instruction. When all are again focused on you, ask for a couple of volunteers to tell what their partners said.

> Just like Cowgirl Kate and Cocoa, you too can help each other by working together. During your writing time, when you are working on your papers at your tables, your partner can help

you in many good ways. What are some ways we may need help during Writer's Workshop?

Listen to responses from a two or three volunteers, and then add your own helpful ideas to the discussion. Ask a child to pretend to be your partner and role-play how a partner can help.

Connection:

Remind children to work quietly with and help their partners.

> Boys and girls, let's work together. Every day I want you to sit quietly beside your partner during our Writer's Workshop lesson. You will turn to your partner when I ask you to and you will discuss what I ask you to discuss. You should look at your partner and listen to what your partner has to say. I expect you to take turns. When I give the signal, you should turn back to face me and be ready to look and listen to learn.
>
> When you return to your table to write, I expect you to help your writing partner if he or she needs help. If you ask your writing partner for help and he or she doesn't know how to help you, you should first ask a nearby neighbor at your table. Remember to stay in your seat. Do not ask someone from another table for help. If your partner cannot help you and your nearby neighbor cannot help you, then you may ask me.
>
> To help you remember whom to ask for help, we will make a chart called, "We Can Ask for Help!"

We Can Ask for Help!

1. We can ask our partner.

2. We can ask our nearby neighbor.

3. We can ask the teacher.

Work together to construct a chart that you can post as a reminder for all to see.

Dismiss children from the group a few at a time and comment on the things you see them doing right as they go back to their seats. You may also use this type of dialogue to lead those children who are more reluctant to begin.

While children are working, conference with them, especially with those who are unsure about how to begin.

Reflection:

Consider this mini-lesson. What worked and what didn't? What would you do differently next year?

_____

_____

_____

_____

Mini-Lesson 11:
Using Supplies Independently

Materials:
∗ Containers for storing writing tools

Objective:
To teach children to use supplies independently

Introduction:
Tell children that have special tools that they use for writing.

> Boys and girls, today I am going to teach you one more thing that writers do. I am going to teach you how to get and take care of the supplies you will need to write.

Instruction:
Teach children how the supply systems will work in your classroom.

> All writers must have something to write with and they need their writing tools nearby so they can write when they have an idea. In this class, you will need to have your supplies close by, so we have very special writer's toolboxes, and in them we have containers just like real authors do on their desks. We have a cup for pencils, and a cup for crayons. We also have empty cups. This week, as we learn how to take care of supplies, we will fill these cups so we will have in each toolbox a cup for colored pencils and a cup for markers. We also have a special place to keep our writing folder. When it is time for writing, we can get our writing folders out quickly, so no one wastes a precious moment of writing time.

Practice:
Demonstrate how the tools should be used, and have children try a practice run.

> Let's pretend it is writing time.
>
> (Act this out.)
>
> I am going back to my table to begin writing. I get a sheet of paper from the writing corner as I go to my table. I sit at my table and get a pencil to write my name, then I sketch—draw quickly—what I am writing about today. Then I write words.
>
> When I am finished with my words, I put my pencil in the pencil cup, with the point down. Next, I use crayons from the crayon cup to add to my picture and to color it. I only take one crayon out of the cup at a time. When I am finished with it, I return it to the cup. I do not have extra crayons rolling around on my table or on the floor. I take care of my supplies. When I am finished with the paper I am working on, I get my writing folder and put my paper in the

folder. I put it on the "finished" side. Then I get another piece of paper to write on. When my teacher calls me to stop, I make sure all my papers are in the right place in my writing folder. I hold my folder and bring it with me when my teachers calls the class to come to our meeting place for Share Time.

Connection:

Tell students that this will be the daily system for using supplies in Writer's Workshop.

> ◼ Boys and girls, this is what we will always do to get ready for writing. It is how we will always take care of our supplies. Now, let me watch as you walk quickly and quietly to your writing spot when I call your name. Don't forget to get paper to write your story on and be thinking of your story idea as you walk back to your spot.

Conference with children while they are working.

Reflection:

Consider this mini-lesson. What worked and what didn't? What would you do differently next year?

_____

_____

_____

_____

Mini-Lesson 12:
Writing the Date

Materials:
* Book about writing in a journal, such as *Pepper's Journal: A Kitten's First Year*, by Stuart Murphy
* Whiteboards, markers, erasers (stored in large plastic zippered bags), one for each child

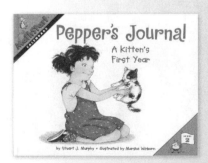

Objective:
To teach children how to write the date on papers

Introduction:
Tell children that they are going to need to keep track of when they write their stories throughout the year. The best way to do this is to write the date on the top of their papers before they begin writing.

■ Writers need to know when they wrote their stories, so they add the date to every story they write. Today I am going to teach you how to add the date to the top of your papers each and every day.

Instruction:

Teach children how to add the date to their stories. Read the book you've selected. For this lesson we use *Pepper's Journal: A Kitten's First Year*.

■ You will add a date to your paper each day just as Lisa does in *Pepper's Journal: A Kitten's First Year*. Why do you think Lisa wrote the date each time she wrote about Pepper?

(Guide children to understand that the date was added so Lisa could remember when each event happened.)

In the same way that Lisa added the date so she could remember when something happened during Pepper's first year, we need to add the date to our stories. That way we can remember when we wrote each of our stories.

Each day I will write the date on the whiteboard. When I do, I want you to look at the numbers I have written and then write those numbers the way I did at the top of your writing paper.

Practice:

Demonstrate how to write today's date, then have children practice. (If this is the first time children have used their whiteboards, you might want to go over instructions for use.)

■ Watch me as I write today's date on my whiteboard. First, I look at the big whiteboard where the date is already written. Next, I pick up my marker and carefully pull the cap off the marker and set the cap down beside my whiteboard. Now I hold my marker and write the first number that I see on the big whiteboard. It is a 9, so I write a 9. The 9 stands for the ninth month of the year. The ninth month of the year is September.

(Count on your fingers as you name off the months.)

This is September. I make a 9. Right after the 9, I make a little straight line called a "dash," like this.

(Demonstrate.)

Now I look for the second number on the big whiteboard. I see a 13. Today is the thirteenth day of September. I write a 13 on my whiteboard. After that, I make another little straight line. Remember, that is called a "dash." Finally, I look for the last number on the big whiteboard. It is 09. It stands for 2009. This is the year 2009. I write 09 on my whiteboard. Now I have written today's date on my whiteboard: 9-13-09.

Now it is time for you to practice writing today's date. Pick up your marker and pull off the cap. Carefully set the cap beside your whiteboard. Now write today's date just as I showed you. First write the 9, then a dash. Next write the 13, then a dash. Last write 09. You have just written today's date! Be sure to take care of your marker. Put the cap on, and make sure you hear the "snap" so you know it won't dry out. Now put your marker down beside your whiteboard.

Connection:

If needed, tell children how to put their whiteboards in the bags and where to store them. Be sure that they understand these are tools for writing and learning, not toys to draw on.

> When I call your table you will take a paper from the paper basket. You will go to your table and write the date for today at the top of your paper just as you did when we practiced on our whiteboards. Then you will write your name. Then you will draw and write about something you like to do, something that is fun for you.

Be prepared to help children individually with the task of adding the date and conference with them while they are working.

Reflection:

Consider this mini-lesson. What worked and what didn't? What would you do differently next year?

_____

_____

_____

_____

Mini-Lesson 13:
Using Markers and Colored Pencils

Materials:

* Book that models using writing supplies appropriately, such as *Purple, Green, and Yellow*, by Robert Munsch, or *How Is a Crayon Made?*, by Oz Charles

* Markers and colored pencils (one cup for each table and an extra cup of each at the writing corner)

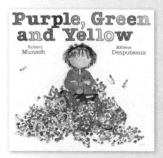

Objective:

To teach children to use markers and colored pencils correctly

Introduction:

Explain that today you want children to learn to use markers and colored pencils correctly.

> Boys and girls, you have been doing such a good job of taking care of your crayons and pencils that I have decided to teach you how to use markers and colored pencils. I will add a cup of markers and a cup of colored pencils to the writing tools at your tables. I will also add colored pencils and markers to our writing corner.

Instruction:

Teach children how to use and care for markers and colored pencils.

> Many illustrators, people who draw pictures for books, like to use markers and colored pencils to make their drawings beautiful. You can also use these tools to make your own wonderful pictures during Writer's Workshop.
>
> When you use markers or colored pencils you will take one out of the cup at a time. You will then put it back in the cup before you get another one. When you use a marker don't press too hard, or you will smash the tip and it won't be any good. When you are finished with a marker, put the lid back on and listen for the "snap." If you don't snap the marker shut, it will dry out and will not work.
>
> When you use a colored pencil, don't press too hard or it may break. When the pencil gets too dull to work anymore, take it to the unsharpened pencil cup and leave it there. Then get a pencil to replace it from the extra supplies.
>
> (Show children where these are located.)
>
> When you use markers, you do need to remember one other very important thing: never mark on anything except your paper unless I tell you it's okay. We never, ever mark on our tables, our clothes, or our bodies with markers.
>
> I'm going to read a book to you about a little girl named Brigid who did not use markers in the right way. When I finish reading, we will talk about what the girl did and what she should have done to use markers correctly. The book about Brigid is called *Purple, Green, and Yellow.*
>
> (Read the book, or read another title you've selected.)

Practice:

Use the book as a springboard to discuss ways to use markers appropriately.

> Brigid did not use her markers in the right way. What did she do wrong? What should she have done? When I say, "Turn to your partner," turn to face your partner and sit knee to knee. Look at your partner and tell your partner what you think Brigid did wrong and what she should have done. When I clap my hands twice and hold a hand up, turn back to face me and look at me. Now turn to your partner.

Give them a minute and then signal them to stop and listen. Then call on two or three children to tell what their partner said.

Connection:

Remind children of your expectations.

> Now that you know how to use your writing and drawing tools correctly, I expect you to take care of them. If you find a marker or a colored pencil out of place, take that marker or colored pencil to the writing corner and put it with the other markers or colored pencils.
>
>   (Show where they are kept.)
>
> If you ever discover that you have lost a marker or a colored pencil, you may go to get one from the writing corner to replace the one you have lost.
>
> Remember, you only take one to replace what you have lost. Never take more. That way we will always have enough in case someone needs them.
>
> Today you may want to use these new art supplies when you return to your seats to draw and write.
>
>   (Call children a few at a time to get paper and go to their seats to work.)

Conference with children while they are working.

Reflection:

Consider this mini-lesson. What worked and what didn't? What would you do differently next year?

_____

_____

_____

_____

Mini-Lesson 14:
Managing the Noise Level

Materials:
* Book that models using quiet voices, such as *Too Much Noise*, by Ann McGovern, or *A Whisper Is Quiet*, by Carolyn Lunn
* Writer's Workshop chart
* Look and Listen to Learn chart

Objective:

Teaching children to keep noise level down during Writer's Workshop

Introduction:

Explain that today you want children to learn how to use quiet voices during Writer's Workshop.

Review the classroom expectations chart and the Look and Listen to Learn chart.

> ■ Boys and girls, you have learned so much about how to act during Writer's Workshop. You also have learned how to look and listen to learn. But there is one thing we still need to work on so that we will always have a good Writer's Workshop time. Sometimes I've noticed that we have too much noise and it is very hard for you to work. Today we're going to work on this problem.

Instruction:

Explain to children that sometimes noise is fine, but inside the classroom during work time, it can interfere with children's learning. That's why it's useful to have guidelines to help everyone remember how much noise is allowed during Writer's Workshop.

> ■ Boys and girls, I have a book to share with you. It made me think of the noise in our classroom. After I read it to you, we are going to talk about noise and we're going to think about when noise is okay and when noise is not okay.
>
> (Read *Too Much Noise*, by Ann McGovern, or another book you've chosen.)

Discuss with children when noise is appropriate and when it is not. For example, noise is fine at a ball game or at recess, but it is not all right when someone is trying to sleep or during an assembly. Lead children to understand that noise is not appropriate during work time because it can make it difficult for others to concentrate or learn.

Next, discuss the level of noise that would be appropriate for Writer's Workshop.

> ■ Would shouting in the classroom be okay? Would calling to your friend across the room be okay? Would talking noisily to the person at the next table be okay?
>
> (If there's any confusion, help children see that these levels of noise are too loud for the classroom during work time.)
>
> These noises are too loud for our classroom. If boys and girls used these voices, the room would be too noisy and I would not be able to teach, and you would not be able to learn. We must use quiet noises. If you are at your table, how quiet must you be so you do not cause problems for me or for your friends?

(Lead children to understand that they need to speak in very quiet voices that do not carry past their tables.)

Boys and girls, some people call these very quiet voices that children use in the classroom "six-inch voices." That means that you cannot hear the person who is speaking if he or she is more than six inches away from you.

(Show children six inches on a ruler.)

This is six inches. That isn't very far. Could you ask your partner a question using a six-inch voice? [Yes] Could you talk with me using a six-inch voice? [Yes] A six-inch voice doesn't bother other people, but we can still use it to get help if we need it.

Practice:

Have students practice using six-inch voices.

- We are going to practice six-inch voices with our partners. When I ask you to, turn to your partner and tell him or her one reason you should use a six-inch voice during Writer's Workshop.

  (Have children practice, and then call on a couple of volunteers to report their partners' answers.)

Connection:

Remind children of your expectations.

- You now know how important it is to use a quiet, six-inch voice during Writer's Workshop. Today and every day when we have work time, I will expect you to use your six-inch voice.

  As I call you to get your paper and go to your seats, I want you to think about how important it is for you to use your quiet voice so we do not have too much noise in our classroom.

  (Call children a few at a time to get paper and go to their seats to work.)

Conference with children while they are working.

Reflection:

Consider this mini-lesson. What worked and what didn't? What would you do differently next year?

_____

_____

_____

_____

Mini-Lesson 15:

Managing Our Noisy Neighbors

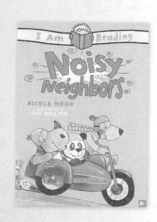

Materials:
* Book that models quiet voices, such as *Noisy Neighbors*, by Nicola Moon
* Chart paper
* Marker

Objective:
To learn more ways to keep the noise level down during Writer's Workshop

Introduction:
Explain that today you want children to learn how to respond if a neighbor is too noisy.

Review the classroom expectations chart and the Look and Listen to Learn chart, if necessary.

> Boys and girls, the last time we met we talked about using six-inch voices during our Writer's Workshop time and many of you really did a great job keeping your voices quiet. But I did notice that some of you were not able to work very well because your neighbor was too noisy. Today I am going to teach you what to do if your neighbor's noise bothers you.

Instruction:
Give children suggestions for dealing with a classmate who is too noisy.

> Sometimes our neighbors are too noisy and we don't know what to do. This book, *Noisy Neighbors*, reminds me of the problem some of you are having.
>
> (Read the book, or another one you've chosen.)
>
> If neighbors are too noisy, there are some things you can do to solve the problem. You can remind your neighbor of the six-inch voice. You can softly ask your neighbor to be quieter or give your neighbor the quiet sign by holding a finger to your lips. You can quietly tell your neighbor that you're working, and then turn away, not looking or answering when he or she talks to you.
>
> If you are the one being noisy and your neighbor reminds you about the rules or gives you the quiet sign, what should you do? You should listen to your friend. You might even say, "Oops! Sorry for being noisy!" Then you should quit being noisy and do your work quietly.

Practice:

Have students volunteer ideas for dealing with a noisy neighbor.

> ■ When I ask you to, turn to your partner and tell him or her one thing you can do if a noisy neighbor is bothering you.
>
> > (Have children discuss, and then call on a few volunteers to report their partners' answers.)

Connection:

Remind children of your expectations.

> ■ You know how important it is to use a quiet, six-inch voice during Writer's Workshop. Now you know what to do if your neighbor is too noisy. Today and every day when we have work time, I will expect you to use your six-inch voice, and I will expect you to know how to remind your neighbors to use quiet voices too.
>
> As I call you to get your paper and go to your seats, I want you to remind yourselves that you are going to use a six-inch voice today and that you are not going to be a noisy neighbor.
>
> > (Call children a few at a time to get paper and go to their seats to work.)

Conference with children while they are working.

Reflection:

Consider this mini-lesson. What worked and what didn't? What would you do differently next year?

_____

_____

_____

_____

Mini-Lesson 16:
Sharing the Teacher

Materials:

* Book that models how to share with others, such as *It's Hard to Share My Teacher*, by Joan Prestine, *It's Mine*, by Leo Lionni, or *Mine! Mine! Mine!*, by Shelly Becker

* Writer's Workshop expectations chart

Objective:

To help children understand that in a classroom with many students, children must take turns speaking with the teacher

Introduction:

Explain to the students that they are going to learn how to share the teacher with their classmates during Writer's Workshop.

> Boys and girls, I've seen you all making an effort to follow the guidelines on our classroom chart. You're doing a great job.
>
> (Review the chart.)
>
> Today I'd like to read a book to you.
>
> (*It's Hard to Share My Teacher* is just right for this lesson, but you can use another favorite if you prefer.)
>
> In this book, the boy has a problem. He likes the teacher. He finds out that his classmates like the teacher, too, and need her help a lot, just like he does. The book will help us in our Writer's Workshop because it seems we may be having some of the same problems this boy has.

Instruction:

Read the book you've selected. After reading, discuss the issues raised in the story:

- What was the boy's problem?
- What did he do to solve his problem?
- Did this solution work?
- Why is it important to take turns?
- Why is it important to "share" the teacher?

Discuss appropriate ways to get and to share the teacher's attention. Encourage children to offer ideas.

> By taking turns and sharing the teacher, our Writer's Workshop will go a lot more smoothly!

Practice:

Determine as a class how the students will let you know they need help.

> What can you do to let me know that you need help?

Have a couple of children answer and lead them to an appropriate response if necessary.

> What will you do if I am busy helping another child and cannot come to you right away? Turn to your partner knee to knee and decide something you could do while you are waiting.

Connection:

Remind students to share the teacher when they are writing today.

■ So writers, today and from now on, let's practice taking turns and sharing the teacher. By doing this, our Writer's Workshop will go much more smoothly.

Let's add one more thing to our How We Act During Writer's Workshop chart: "We share our teacher. While we are waiting, we add to our picture or words or start another paper."

Conference with children as they work quietly at their desks.

Reflection:

Consider this mini-lesson. What worked and what didn't? What would you do differently next year?

_____

_____

_____

_____

How We Act During Writer's Workshop

1. We walk quickly and quietly to our meeting place.

2. We sit quietly in our spots.

3. We listen to our partners when we share.

4. We take care of our pencils and crayons.

5. We watch our teacher and what she is showing us.

6. We listen when the teacher is talking to us.

7. We raise our hands to give an answer.

8. We share our teacher. While we are waiting, we add to our picture or words or start another paper.

You should be well on your way to establishing a flourishing learning environment for Writer's Workshop. With your classroom management in place, you will be ready to maximize the learning that will occur throughout the following units. Are there still areas you need to work on for your Writer's Workshop to be a success? If so, take time to ensure routines are running smoothly.

Unit 3: Concepts of Print

Depending on your students, a few, some, or most of your children will be unfamiliar with basic concepts of print. Even those who have some familiarity can certainly benefit from a review. The mini-lessons in Unit 3 introduce such essential concepts as the use of uppercase and lowercase letters, and the organization of print from top to bottom and left to right. If students need more practice or exposure, repeat these lessons on subsequent days.

Mini-Lesson 17:
Identifying What Letters Are

Materials:
* A favorite alphabet book, such as *Shiver Me Letters: A Pirate ABC*, by June Sobel

* Paper

Objective:
To make sure children know what letters are and that we find them everywhere

Introduction:
Explain to the students what you want them to learn today—that letters are parts of words that represent what we say.

> Writers, you have been drawing and telling lots of stories through your pictures. I'm glad to see so many wonderful pictures, or illustrations. I'm also glad to see so many of you writing letters and words to go with your illustrations. Today, we're going to talk more about how letters can help us write.

Instruction:
Introduce the alphabet book and show how the author uses the letters. For this lesson, we use *Shiver Me Letters*.

> Today we are going to read the book *Shiver Me Letters,* by June Sobel. It will help us notice more things about the alphabet and how that can help us with writing.
>
> (Read the book, showing students the illustrations as you go.)

Practice:
Use the book as a springboard for a discussion, asking questions about letters.

> What is the alphabet?
> Where can we find the alphabet?

Why do we have an alphabet?
How many letters are in the alphabet?
What are some of the letters in the alphabet?
What can we do with the alphabet?
How does the alphabet help us?
What do the letters sound like?
How many letters are in your name?
How many letters are in my name?
Where do we find letters?

Connection:

Remind students that they use the letters of the alphabet every day when they write during Writer's Workshop.

> ■ You know a lot about letters! That's good, because we will be using letters a lot this year! We are going to talk about letters more in the next few Writer's Workshops. From now on, use letters in your writing to help you write your stories.

Conference with children while they are working.

Share Time:

Gather children together again, and ask one student to read his or her drawing/writing to the rest of the class.

Reflection:

Consider this mini-lesson. What worked and what didn't? What would you do differently next year?

_____

_____

_____

_____

Mini-Lesson 18:
Identifying the Difference Between Uppercase and Lowercase Letters

Materials:

* Book that models big and little (for uppercase and lowercase) letters, such as *Big Pig and Little Pig*, by David McPhail, *Big Dog . . . Little Dog*, by P. D. Eastman, or *Big Al and Shrimpy*, by Andrew Clements
* Big books (one for each set of partners)
* Blue and yellow sticky notes
* Chart with headings "UPPER-CASE" and "lowercase"
* Paper

Objective:

To help students distinguish between uppercase and lowercase letters and realize that lowercase letters are used more often

Introduction:

Explain to children that you want them to start using more letters in their writing.

> Yesterday we talked about letters. Today we're going to talk more about letters, and the book we're going to read will help us with finding problems in our writing.

Instruction:

Introduce the book you've chosen. For this lesson, we use *Big Pig and Little Pig*.

> Today we are going to read the book *Big Pig and Little Pig*, by David McPhail. After reading this book we will be able to figure out what kind of letter—uppercase or lowercase—to use in our writing.
>
> (Read *Big Pig and Little Pig*, showing students the illustrations as you go.)

Practice:

Discuss the book. After reading the story, generate a discussion about how the characters were similar and different. Then discuss how letters are similar and different.

> Why do we have big and little letters in our alphabet? Just like Big Pig and Little Pig were different, the big and little letters in our alphabet are different. The big letters are called "uppercase letters" and the little letters are called "lowercase letters." We use both kinds when we write. What kind of letters do you think we use more of when we write—uppercase or lowercase letters?
>
> (Discuss as a group.)
>
> Let's find out if writers use more uppercase or more lowercase letters when they write.

Give one Big Book to each set of partners. Ask students to look for uppercase and lowercase letters in their Big Book. Ask students to choose one page and count the uppercase letters they see, and write that number on a yellow sticky note. Then ask them to count the lowercase letters on the same page and write that number on a blue sticky note. Gather as a class and allow each pair to share their findings. Display the sticky notes on the board under the headings "UPPERCASE" and "lowercase." Help children come to the conclusion that writers use more lowercase letters than uppercase letters.

Connection:

Tell students that we will use uppercase and lowercase letters of the alphabet every day as we write during Writer's Workshop.

> Today I saw many of you write letters and words to go with
> your pictures. What kind of letters did you use, uppercase or
> lowercase?

Conference with children while they are working.

Share Time:

When children have gathered together again, ask one student to read his or her drawing/writing to the rest of the class.

Reflection:

Consider this mini-lesson. What worked and what didn't? What would you do differently next year?

_____

_____

_____

_____

_____

Mini-Lesson 19:
Matching Uppercase and Lowercase Letters

Materials:
* Book that models matching uppercase letters to lowercase, letters, such as *Chicka Chicka Boom Boom*, by Bill Martin, Jr., or *Little Old Big Beard* and *Big Young Little Beard*, by Remy Charlip
* Highlighter tape in two different colors
* Letter cards with uppercase and lowercase letters

Objective:
To help students match uppercase and lowercase letters and know the difference between them

Introduction:
Explain to children that you want them to match uppercase and lowercase letters.

> Boys and girls, you have been drawing and writing stories.
> Yesterday we talked about the difference between uppercase
> and lowercase letters. Today we're going to talk more about
> uppercase and lowercase letters.

Instruction:

Introduce the book you've chosen. For this lesson, we use *Chicka Chicka Boom Boom*.

> Today we are going to read the book *Chicka Chicka Boom Boom*, by Bill Martin, Jr. It will help us notice more things about the alphabet.
>
> (Read the book, showing students the illustrations as you go.)

Practice:

Use *Chicka Chicka Boom Boom* as a springboard to discuss how the letters of the alphabet are similar and different.

> Why do we have uppercase and lowercase letters in our alphabet?

Play an alphabet matching game by asking children to find each letter's match (uppercase and lowercase matches). Return to the text and ask students to help you find lowercase letters in the text and highlight them with highlighter tape in one color. Next, have the students find uppercase letters in the text and highlight them with highlighter tape in the other color.

Connection:

Remind the students that we will use uppercase and lowercase letters of the alphabet every day as we write during Writer's Workshop.

> Remember that letters are either uppercase or lowercase. Today and from now on, we will use uppercase and lowercase letters as we write in our Writer's Workshop.

Conference with children while they are working.

Share Time:

When children have gathered together again, ask one student to read his or her drawing/writing to the rest of the class.

> Today I saw many of you write letters and words to go with your pictures. What kind of letters did you use, uppercase or lowercase letters?

Reflection:

Consider this mini-lesson. What worked and what didn't? What would you do differently next year?

_____

_____

_____

_____

_____

Mini-Lesson 20:
Top and Bottom

Materials:
- Book that models the concepts of top and bottom, such as *Tops & Bottoms,* by Janet Stevens
- Chart paper
- Marker
- Assorted books
- Paper

Objective:
To help children understand that writing should start at the top of the page and end at the bottom of the page

Introduction:
Explain that today you want children to start writing at the top of a page and end at the bottom of the page.

> Boy and girls, you have been drawing and writing stories. I'm glad to see so many good illustrations. Yesterday we talked about the difference between uppercase and lowercase letters and matched the uppercase letters to the lowercase letters. Today we're going to talk about how we start at the top of a page when we write and end at the bottom of the page.

Instruction:
Introduce your chosen book. For this lesson, we use *Tops & Bottoms.*

> Today I will teach you that writing should start at the top of a page and end at the bottom.
>
> (Read *Tops & Bottoms,* showing students the illustrations as you go.)
>
> Now, I am going to write a story, and I want you to pay attention to where I start on my page.
>
> (Write a short story, making sure you clearly start at the top of the page, and write until you reach the bottom. You'll probably want to have a story already in mind to ensure that it fits, top to bottom, on one page. When you're finished, ask students to show you where you started writing on the page.)
>
> Did I start at the bottom of the page? Did I start in the middle of the page?
>
> (Write "TOP" at the top of the page.)
>
> Where did I stop my story? Did I stop at the top of the page? Did I stop in the middle?
>
> (Write "BOTTOM" at the bottom of the page.)

Practice:

Identify top and bottom on pages of a book.

> ■ I am going to give you and your partner a book to look at, and I want you to decide where the top is on each page and where the bottom is on each page.
>
> (Hand out books for children to look at in order to identify top and bottom.)

Connection:

Remind children to begin writing at the top of the page and to end at bottom of the page when they write from now on. (Of course, you may wish to point out that not all student writing will be long enough to extend to the bottom of the page.)

> ■ Boys and girls, today and from now on when you write, I want you to begin at the top of the page. If you write a lot, you should end your writing at the bottom of the page before starting on a new page.

Conference with children while they are working.

Share Time:

Gather children together again and ask one student to read his or her drawing/writing to the rest of the class.

Ask the students to turn knee to knee and talk with their partner about what they noticed about his or her work.

Reflection:

Consider this mini-lesson. What worked and what didn't? What would you do differently next year?

_____

_____

_____

_____

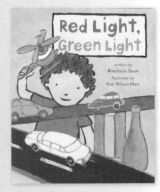

Mini-Lesson 21:
Left and Right

Materials:

* Book that models directionality, such as *Red Light, Green Light*, by Anastasia Suen, or *Left or Right?*, by Karl Rehm

* Chart paper
* Marker
* Red and green dot stickers

Objective:
To help students understand that as they write, their hand moves across the page from left to right

Introduction:
Explain to students that today you want them to learn that when they write, they should start on left side of the page and continue across to the right side.

■ Yesterday we talked about how we start at the top of the page and end at the bottom of the page. Today, we are going to learn about starting on the left side of your page and moving across to the right side.

Instruction:
Introduce the book you've selected. For this lesson, we use *Red Light, Green Light*.

■ Today I will teach you that when you are writing you should always start at the left side of the page and move across to the right side of the page.

(Read the book.)

What does it mean when you see a green light? Yes, it means "go." When we write, we always start at the left side of the page. I am going to put a green sticker here at the left side of my paper. It lets me know I need to start, or GO, here on the left side as I begin my writing.

What does a red light mean? Right, it means "stop." When we write, we STOP on the right side of the page. Then we make a "return sweep" and GO again at the left side of the page. Then we continue with GO, STOP, return sweep, GO, STOP, return sweep, until we are finished with our writing. Since we STOP at the right side of our paper, I am going to put a red sticker there. It shows me that I need to STOP at the right side of my paper with my writing.

Watch as I write a story. Notice where I start and stop.

(Write a short story on a sheet of chart paper, making sure you are clearly starting at the top of the page and on the left side of the paper. Emphasize starting, stopping, and the return sweep, as you are writing.)

Practice:
Identify left and right on the pages of a book.

■ What did you notice as I wrote my story? Where did I start my writing?

(Discuss.)

Did I write downward? Did I write upward? That's right, I started at the left and wrote toward the right side of the paper.

> ▪ Where did I put my green sticker? Why did I put it there?
>
>   [On the left, to signal start.]
>
>   Where is my red sticker? Why did I put it there?
>
>   [On the right, to signal stop.]

Give each student a sheet of paper, a red sticker, and a green sticker.

> ▪ Put the green sticker on the side of the paper where you will start your writing. Put the red sticker on the side of the paper where you will stop each line of writing. When you write today and from now on, remember that you always start on the left side of your paper and write across the page to the right side of the paper.

Connection:

Remind the students to begin writing on the left side of a paper and move across the page to the right.

> ▪ Writers, today and from now on when you write, you will begin on the left of the page and move across to the right side of the page.

Conference with children while they are working.

Share Time:

When children have gathered together again, ask one student to read his or her drawing/writing to the rest of the class. Ask the students to turn knee to knee and talk with their partner about what they noticed about that student's work.

Reflection:

Consider this mini-lesson. What worked and what didn't? What would you do differently next year?

_____

_____

_____

_____

Mini-Lesson 22:
Putting Letters Together to Make Words

Materials:
* Book that models putting letters together to make words, such as *The Alphabet Keeper*, by Mary Murphy, or *Mouse Makes Words*, by Kathryn Heling
* Letter magnets or letter cards for *a, t, c, b, h*
* Pocket chart or magnet board

Objective:

To enable students to spell simple words using more than one letter

Introduction:

Explain to the students that today you want them to understand that writers put letters together to make words.

> Yesterday we talked about how we start writing at the left side of the paper and write across the page to the right side. Today we are going to learn about how to put letters together to make words when we write.

Instruction:

Give each student a magnetic whiteboard and the magnetic letters *a, t, c, b, h.* Alternatively, you can use letter cards.

> Does anyone know how to spell *cat*?
>
>> (Allow children some time to use their magnetic letters to make the word *cat.* Continue with other simple words such as *at, hat, bat,* and so on.)
>
> I noticed when you were spelling these words that you used more than one letter. Why did you use more than one letter to spell these words?
>
>> (Help students come to the conclusion that words are spelled with more than one letter, except the words *a* and *I.*)
>
> Today's book will help us better understand how we put letters together to make words.

Practice:

Read the book you chose for this lesson.

> In this book, what did we learn about letters?
>
>> (Start a discussion about what children learned. Help them come to the conclusion that letters work together to make words. Practice making words using the following letter magnets or cards: *a, t, c, b, h: at cat bat hat.*)

Connection:

Remind the students to use the letters of the alphabet every day as they write during Writer's Workshop and that all letters work together to make words.

> Writers, today and from now on when you write, you will put together letters to make words when you are writing.

Conference with children while they are working.

Share Time:

When children have gathered together again, ask one student to read his or her drawing/writing to the rest of the class. Ask the students to turn knee to knee and talk with their partner about what they noticed about that student's work.

Reflection:

Consider this mini-lesson. What worked and what didn't? What would you do differently next year?

_____

_____

_____

_____

_____

By now, you probably have your classroom management in place. Are there specific children who are hindering the success of your Writer's Workshop? Have you conferenced with them regarding their behavior? What else can you do?

Unit 4: Labeling

One of the simplest forms of writing is labeling. In this unit, we explore labels across several mini-lessons. Using sample books and items in the classroom, you'll identify labels, explain to children when and why authors and others use them, and then give children practice making some labels themselves. Repeat any of the lessons as needed to give students additional practice.

Mini-Lesson 23:
What Are Labels, and What Do They Look Like?

Materials:
* Book in which illustrations are labeled, such as *Of Colors and Things*, by Tana Hoban, *Cassie's Word Quilt*, by Faith Ringgold, *Eating the Alphabet*, by Lois Ehlert, or *Feathers for Lunch*, by Lois Ehlert
* Big Book or poster-size picture with items labeled
* Highlighting tape

Objective:
To help children identify labels in books

Introduction:
Explain that today you are going to show children some wonderful books that have beautiful illustrations that the authors have labeled. Hold up one or more books in which the authors have labeled the illustrations.

> Boys and girls, today I am going to show you some books. In these books the authors have written words by the pictures to tell what the pictures are. We call these words labels.

Instruction:
Give several examples of labels used in your selected book.

> I would like you to notice this book by Lois Ehlert. It is called *Eating the Alphabet*. In this book, I see pictures of fruits and vegetables with words beside them. These words are labels.
>
> (Show additional books, if desired, and discuss the labels.)
>
> Many authors use labels in their books. We recognize labels because they are usually just one or two words written near a picture.

Practice:
Have students highlight labels on a Big Book (if you have one available) or on a large picture you have prepared.

We are going to find labels on this page of *Eating the Alphabet*. We will use highlighting tape, which is a special kind of tape that won't hurt the book. We would never do anything to hurt a book!

If you see a label on this page, raise your hand quietly. I will not be able to call on all of you, but I will choose as many as I can.

(Proceed to call on four or five children to identify and highlight labels on the page you have chosen.)

Connection:

Remind children that they can use labels in their writing, too.

Today when you write you can use labels, just like the author did.

Remember that as you work, it is important to use a quiet, six-inch voice during Writer's Workshop. Now, get your paper as I call your table and walk quietly back to your seats and do what good writers do.

(Call children a few at a time to get paper and go to their seats to work.)

Conference with children while they are working.

Reflection:

Consider this mini-lesson. What worked and what didn't? What would you do differently next year?

_____

_____

_____

_____

_____

Mini-Lesson 24:
Why Do We Use Labels, and What Can We Label?

Materials:
* Books that feature labels (see Mini-Lesson 23 for suggestions)
* Photocopies of a picture with most items labeled, and a few items unlabeled
* Pencils
* Clipboards, one per child

Objective:

To identify labels and understanding their purpose

Introduction:

Explain that today you are going to look at another book that has beautiful illustrations the author has labeled. You are going to think about what kinds of things authors can label, and why labels are useful.

Hold up one or more books in which the authors have labeled the illustrations. For this lesson, we use *Of Colors and Things*, by Tana Hoban.

> ■ Boys and girls, sometimes you will find books like these in which the author has used labels. We looked at labels when we met last. Today we are going to talk about why authors use labels and we are going to look at the kinds of things authors can label.

Instruction:

Give several examples of labels used in books. Explain when and why labels are used.

> ■ Look at this book by Tana Hoban. Its title is *Of Colors and Things*. Notice that this author also used labels. She used labels to tell what the pictures are. That's what authors do. They use labels to tell about the pictures, to tell what the pictures are. Have you noticed that the authors of the books we have looked at have labeled all sorts of things? You can label anything.

Practice:

Give each child a clipboard, a pencil, and a copy of a picture that has several items labeled and a few items that are not labeled. Ask them to circle the labels. Then ask them to find one thing in the picture that they can label.

> ■ We are going to find labels on this page. I am going to give each of you a tray (clipboard) with a pencil and a paper like this on it! You will find all of the labels you can and you will circle them with your pencil. Then you will find something that has not been labeled. You will write a label for that thing.
>
> (When they are finished, have four or five children share their labels.)

Connection:

Remind children that they can use labels when they write, too.

> ■ Remember that today when you write, you can use labels also, just like these authors did.
>
> Now, get your paper as I call your table and walk quietly back to your seats and do what good writers do.
>
> (Call children a few at a time to get paper and go to their seats to work.)

Conference with children while they are working.

Reflection:
Consider this mini-lesson. What worked and what didn't? What would you do differently next year?

_____

_____

_____

_____

Mini-Lesson 25:
A Picture Dictionary Has Labels

Materials:
* Picture dictionaries, such as *The Best Word Ever,* by Richard Scarry, or Scholastic *Children's Dictionary*—one for each pair, if possible

Objective:
To show children that picture dictionaries can be used to find names for things

Introduction:
Show children the dictionaries and explain that these can be used when they are writing to help them find words.

> Boys and girls, we have been talking a lot about labels. We know what labels are and what they look like. We know labels are used to name things, and we know that we can label anything. Today, I'm going to show you a very useful book called a dictionary. (Hold up one of the dictionaries.) This dictionary has all kinds of pictures in it, and each picture has a label. I can use this dictionary to find words that I may not know how to write.

Instruction:
Show several examples of the pictures and labels in a picture dictionary.

> If I would like to find the word *mouse*, I would look through the dictionary until I found a picture of a mouse. If I know that *mouse* starts with an *m* it is easier for me to find the picture, because the dictionary is put together in ABC order with *a* words in the very front and *z* words in the very back. So, if I know my ABCs, I know *m* is in the middle. If I look in the middle of the dictionary, I should be able to find words that start with *m*, like the word *mouse*.

(Give additional examples until you can see that most of the children understand the concept.)

Practice:

Give each pair a dictionary. Have them look up words of interest to them. Then have them look up some words that you call out.

■ You will work with your partner to find words in a dictionary. Hold the dictionary between you and use it together to find words you would like to see.

(Allow a few minutes for children to explore the dictionaries.)

Now, I would like you and your partner to find the word that I say. Listen carefully and think about the sound you hear at the beginning of the word. Then think about the letter for that sound. Think about ABC order, and think about where that letter would be in the alphabet. Is it toward the beginning? If so, it will be toward the beginning of the dictionary. Is it toward the end? Then it will be toward the end of the dictionary. See if you can find this word.

(Give a word that is in the dictionary. Repeat with a few more.)

Connection:

Remind children that they can use the dictionaries to find words they want to write.

■ Remember that today when you write, you can use your dictionaries to find words that you might want to write but aren't sure how to spell. Now, as I call you and your partner, take your dictionary, get your paper, and walk quietly back to your seats to begin your work.

(Call children a few at a time to get paper and go to their seats to work.)

Conference with children while they are working.

Reflection:

Consider this mini-lesson. What worked and what didn't? What would you do differently next year?

_____

_____

_____

_____

_____

Mini-Lesson 26:
We Can Label Things in Our Classroom

Materials:
* Sentence strips or index cards   * Tape
* Markers

Objective:
To show students that items in the classroom can be labeled

Introduction:
You have been learning a lot about labels. Today we are going to label things in our classroom.

> Boys and girls, you know a lot about labels. You know what labels are and what they look like. You know we use labels to tell what things are, and you know we can label anything. Today we are going to label things in our classroom.

Instruction:
Have students volunteer items in the classroom to label, then write the names of those items on sentence strips or index cards and tape the labels to the items selected.

> I am looking in our classroom, and I see a bulletin board. I am going to make a label for "bulletin board," then tape the label to the bulletin board. Would you help me figure out how to write *bulletin board* on this strip of paper? Let's see. *Bulletin board* is two words. We will start with the first word, *bulletin*. What sound do you hear at the beginning of *bulletin*? What letter do I write for that sound?
>
> (Have children help you spell *bulletin board* and then tape the label to the bulletin board. Then have them take turns volunteering other classroom items to label. Label four or five items in the classroom.)

Practice:
Give each child an index card or a portion of a sentence strip. Tell children that they are each going to write a label to attach to an item in the classroom. Younger children may need to work with partners.

> I am going to give each of you a card. Think of an item in the classroom that you would like to label. When you get the card, write your label on it, and then I will help you tape it to the object.

Allow a few minutes for children to write their labels, then give them tape and help them put the labels up around the room. It's fine to have more than one label for an object.

Connection:
Remind children that they can use labels when they write.

■ Remember that you can use labels when you draw and write, and you can use your dictionaries to find words that you might want to write but aren't sure how to spell.

Also remember that as you work, it is important to use a quiet, six-inch voice, so you do not bother other writers. Now, as I call your table, get your paper and walk quietly back to your seats to begin your work.

(Call children a table at a time to get paper and go to their seats to work.)

Conference with children while they are working.

Reflection:

Consider this mini-lesson. What worked and what didn't? What would you do differently next year?

_____

_____

_____

_____

Mini-Lesson 27:
We Can Label a Picture

Materials:
* Large picture (an image from an old calendar works well)
* Picture duplicated on copier paper (one for each pair)
* Markers
* Pencils

Objective:
To show children that they can label items in a picture.

Introduction:
Tell children that today they will practice labeling pictures.

■ Boys and girls, you know a lot about labels. You know what labels are and what they look like. You know we use labels to tell what things are and you know we can label anything. Today we are going to label pictures.

Instruction:
Display a large picture on your easel. You may want to laminate it so that you can write directly on the picture, or tape it to the center of a

sheet of chart paper and write the labels on the paper. Discuss the picture. Then choose an item in the picture to label and write the label on the chart paper. You might want to draw an arrow from the label to the item in the picture.

> ■ I have a picture and I would like to label some of the things I see in it. This picture shows _____. I see a _____ in the picture. I would like to label it, so I will use my marker to write the word.
>
>   (Write the label.)
>
> Now, I will draw an arrow from my label to the item in the picture.
>
>   (Have children help you label some additional items in the picture. Label four or five items.)

Practice:

Give each pair a picture photocopied on white paper. Have children work together to write labels for things they see in the picture.

> ■ You are going to work with your partner to label the things you see in this picture. Be sure to work together to label as many things as you can.
>
>   (Allow a few minutes for children to write their labels, and then have four or five children share the labels they wrote.)

Connection:

Remind children that they can use labels when they write.

> ■ Remember that you can use labels when you draw and write, and you can use your dictionaries to find words that you want to write but aren't sure how to spell.
>
> Now, as I call your table, get your paper and walk quietly back to your seats to begin your work.
>
>   (Call children a table at a time to get paper and go to their seats to work.)

Conference with children while they are working.

Reflection:

Consider this mini-lesson. What worked and what didn't? What would you do differently next year?

_____

_____

_____

_____

_____

Mini-Lesson 28:

I Can Draw My Own Picture and Write My Own Labels

Materials:
- ∗ Large sheet of paper (writing paper used for teacher modeling)
- ∗ Markers

Objective:

To show children how to label their own pictures

Introduction:

Congratulate children on the great job they are doing with labels. Tell them that today they will practice drawing and labeling their own pictures.

> ■ Wow, you have really learned a lot about labels. Today, you will draw your own pictures and write your own labels.

Instruction:

Place a large sheet of chart paper on your easel. On it draw a picture and label it.

> ■ Today I am going to think of a story that I would like to tell. I would like to write about something I did last weekend. Last weekend I went kite flying. I'm going to draw a quick picture to show you my story.
>
> (Very quickly sketch your story on the large sheet of paper. Be sure to add enough details so you will have plenty of things to label.)
>
> Now I'm going to label my picture. Let's see, I think I'll label the kite. I'm going to say "kite" slowly to hear all of the sounds. I hear /k/ sound at the beginning of the word *kite*. That sound is made with the letter *k*, so I will write the letter *k* at the beginning of my word.
>
> (Continue to talk aloud as you write and label additional items.)

Practice:

Allow children the opportunity to help you label a few more items in your picture.

> ■ Would you help me label just a few more things?
>
> (Have children volunteer words and help spell them. If children are able, you might have them write the labels. Ask for two or three volunteers.)
>
> Now, help me write a sentence or two to tell my story.
>
> (Very quickly write a couple of sentences, having children volunteer letters for the sounds they hear.)

Connection:

Remind children that they can use labels when they write.

■ Today, draw a picture and write labels for things in the picture. Then you may write your story below the picture.

Now, as I call your table, get your paper and walk quietly back to your seats to begin your work.

(Call children one table at a time to get paper and go to their seats to work. If needed, remind them to use their six-inch voices.)

Conference with children while they are working

Reflection:

Consider this mini-lesson. What worked and what didn't? What would you do differently next year?

_____

_____

_____

_____

UNIT 5: MECHANICS OF THE WRITING PROCESS

The mini-lessons in this brief unit will help you introduce a few basic mechanics of the writing process. We focus on some introductory spelling strategies, such as referring to an alphabet chart and listening for beginning sounds before writing each word. We end this unit with a low-pressure mini-lesson that essentially encourages students to do their best but not to worry *too* much about correct spelling. There will be plenty of time in their school careers to perfect their spelling. For now, we want them to not get too bogged down with correctness—and simply to write!

Mini-Lesson 29:
Using the Alphabet Chart

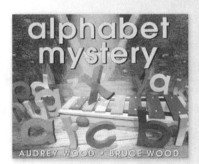

Materials:
* * Alphabet book, such as *Alphabet Mystery*, by Audrey Wood
* * A classroom alphabet chart

Objective:
To have students identify the alphabet chart and understand that it can help with letter names and sounds

Introduction:
Discuss uses of the alphabet chart with the students.

> ■ Writers, we have been learning about letters. Today we are going to read a book about the letters of the alphabet. Something has happened, and Little x is missing. The other letters work to solve the mystery of its disappearance.

Instruction:
Read *Alphabet Mystery* or another alphabet book and discuss the importance of letters.

> ■ How and why are letters useful?
> What do we use letters for?

Practice:
Ask the students to look for letters around the classroom.

> ■ Boys and girls, if you look around the room, you might find letters on the walls and other things in our room. Can you tell me where you find letters in our room?

> (Allow a few answers, making sure the ABC chart is mentioned among the answers.)

Connection:

Tell students that they can always look at the ABC chart as they write to help them with their letters.

> ■ This is the ABC chart. We have an ABC chart in our room to help us with letter names and sounds. We will use the ABC chart when we are writing this year. It can help us with letters as we write.

Reflection:

Consider this mini-lesson. What worked and what didn't? What would you do differently next year?

_____

_____

_____

_____

Mini-Lesson 30:
Stretching and Writing Words

Materials:
* Chart paper
* Story idea, with illustrations already drawn on two pages
* Marker
* Pile of familiar books that have pictures and words
* Individual whiteboards, markers, and erasers

Objective:

To teach students that they need to separate the sounds they hear in each word and write down the letters that correspond to those sounds

Introduction:

Tell children that you are going to teach them how to stretch out the sounds of a word and write each letter they hear.

> ■ Boys and girls, today I am going to show you how I decide what letters to put on the page when I'm writing my words.

Instruction:

Write a story in front of the students, demonstrating what you want them to try in their writing.

Earlier I decided to write about a raft I went on, so on this page I drew the raft floating. Now, I'm going to write my story in front of you. Watch how I write my words.

I think I'll write, "I went on a raft." Okay, *I.* That's easy.

    (Write "I.")

Now *went.*

    (Break the word down as you write it.) /W/ *w.*

    (Reread with your finger under the letters *I* and *w* and then progress to e-n-t.)

Now I need -ent: *e* and *n* and *t* at the end.

    (Write and reread again.)

"I went."

Did you notice that I first said what I wanted to write, then I broke it down to just the first word, and then I wrote and reread that? Then I said the next word, I broke down the sounds. And I wrote each sound, and then I reread again.

Practice:

Ask the students to join you in writing the sounds they hear in the words you write.

Will you help me to keep going? First I'll reread what I wrote. Let's do that together.

    (Wait for the class and together, with your finger under the print, read, "I went.")

Now let's say and write what's next: *on.* On your hands

    (Point to your palm.)

pretend to write that word, and I'll do it up here.

    (Write *on.* Then write *a.*)

Now what do we do? We reread, don't we? Let's do it together. "I went on a..."

Raft!

    (Point to the place on the paper where you will write *raft* and move your hands as you say the word slowly and fluidly.)

Say it with me. We are stretching the word like a rubber band.

    (Say it together a few times.)

What sound do you hear first? /r/? Okay. We hear the /r/ sound and that is spelled with an *r.* Next we hear an /a/ sound, which is written with an *a.* Next, what do we hear? The /f/ sound. So we write the letter *f.* Finally, we hear a /t/ sound. That is written with a *t.* Let's reread the sentence.

Connection:

Ask the students to try on their own what you just modeled for them.

> ■ Today, boys and girls, try to write words on your page, just like the authors do. Say the words, stretch them out, then write what you hear. Reread and say more.

Conference with children while they are working.

Share Time:

Gather children together again, and ask one student to read his or her drawing/writing to the class. Ask students to turn knee to knee and talk with their partner about what they noticed about that student's work.

Reflection:

Consider this mini-lesson. What worked and what didn't? What would you do differently next year?

_____

_____

_____

_____

_____

Mini-Lesson 31:
Listening for and Writing Beginning Sounds

Materials:
* Chart paper   * Marker

Objective:

To help students notice beginning sounds so that they can get those initial letters down on the paper

Introduction:

Explain to students that they are writing like authors. Tell them that you are going to teach them how to stretch out the sounds of a word and write each letter they hear, especially the initial letter.

> ■ Boys and girls, we've been talking about stretching out words so that we can hear the sounds in them. Today I want to show you how to get the initial sounds you hear in your words down on the paper.

Instruction:

Take out a piece of writing you've used previously in a mini-lesson and tell students that you want to add some more to it. Tell children to watch as you model how to write the words on the page.

■ Watch me say the words and write down the sounds I hear. Later I'm going to ask you to help me. Today I'm going to add to my story about flying my kite. I want to add "The sky was blue."

Hmm. *Sky.* Let me say the word and write down what I hear in the beginning: /s/. I hear an *s.* Let me say it again and listen to what else I hear. What can I hear at the beginning of the word? I hear an *s.* Let me write that down.

(Continue saying, writing, rereading, until finished with the word. Restate the process you used to record your words. Tell students to use the same process when they are writing.)

Boys and girls, did you notice I said the word and wrote down what I heard at the start of the word? Then I said the word again and wrote down what I heard next. I'm telling you that because you can do the same thing.

Practice:

Assign them a word and ask them to try the process with you.

■ Let's try it together with the word *blue.* Say the word *blue.* What do you hear at the beginning?"

(Write the letter.)

There are more sounds in *blue.* Everyone say the word and listen for more sounds.

(Write the letter or letters volunteered.)

Connection:

Remind the students of today's lesson so that they can carry it into their writing. Tell them to get started by listening for the beginning sounds of words, then to listen for more.

■ Today, when you are writing your words, make sure that you say the word once and write down what you hear at the beginning, and then say the word again and write down the other sounds you hear."

Conference with children while they are working.

Share Time:

Gather children together again, and ask one student to read his or her drawing/writing to the rest of the class. Ask the students to turn knee to knee and talk with their partner about what they noticed about that student's work.

Reflection:
Consider this mini-lesson. What worked and what didn't? What would you do differently next year?

_____

_____

_____

_____

Mini-Lesson 32:
Spelling Our Best and Not Worrying About It

Materials:
* Chart paper
* Drawing, prepared in advance
* Marker
* Whiteboards, markers, and erasers for students

Objective:
To show children that their approximate spellings are fine for now and will help them write more

Introduction:
Remind students that they already know how to draw the best they can and keep going. Tell them that they can do the same thing with words.

> A few days ago we talked about drawing the best we can and not worrying if we felt like we couldn't do it. When we don't know how to draw our topics we say, "I'll draw my best," and we know we'll get better because we are working on it.

Instruction:
Model hesitating when you come to a word you don't know how to spell. Try to spell a hard word and then continue on to write more.

> Today I want to write words to go with the picture I drew of a picnic. I want you to watch what I do when I get to tricky words.
>
> (Show the drawing you've prepared.)
>
> "I ate an orange." Hmm, orange. That's hard. I think I'll write _o-r-a-n-j_.
>
> (Talk and write, moving quickly, every now and then hemming and hawing about how to spell a word, but then shrugging and going on.)
>
> Oh well, I'll leave it like that for now and keep going.

Practice:

Point out to the students what you wanted them to notice as you were writing. Invite them to help you go through the process again.

> ■ Did you see how I just did the best I could and kept going? I'm going to have you get your whiteboards so you can join me in doing this for the next page.
>
> (Have children quickly get their whiteboards, markers, and erasers. Then continue with a second page, having children write difficult words on their whiteboards to help you.)
>
> Look how much you got down! Let's read what we've written. Everyone put your finger under the word. Let's read it and keep going.

Connection:

Remind the students that they can do this when they are writing.

> ■ Today, remember, if you want to put something on the paper and you aren't sure how to draw it or how to write it—just do the best you can and keep going.

Conference with children while they are working.

Share Time:

Gather children together again and ask one student to read his or her drawing/writing to the rest of the class. Ask the students to turn knee to knee and talk with their partner about what they noticed about that student's work.

Reflection:

Consider this mini-lesson. What worked and what didn't? What would you do differently next year?

_____

_____

_____

_____

Unit 6: Tools to Help Us Write

The mini-lessons in this unit will help you give students useful tools to develop their writing so they can say what they want to say in print. With the lessons that follow you'll help them plan their writing, demonstrate the importance of leaving spaces between words, and help them stretch words to hear each sound before they write. You'll introduce the word wall and give them some handy word lists to help them spell colors, numbers, days and months, and classmates' names—to boost their vocabularies.

Mini-Lesson 33:
Planning Our Writing

Materials:

* A book about working together, such as *If You Give a Mouse a Cookie*, by Laura Numeroff
* Chart paper, with a picture already sketched on one sheet
* Marker

Objective:

To have children plan a sentence and write it

Introduction:

Congratulate children on the great job they've been doing and the many things they have learned about writing, and introduce the day's lesson: planning before writing.

> Boys and girls, you have learned a lot about writing already this year! Today you're going to write your own sentence.

Instruction:

First, read the book you've selected. (For this lesson we use *If You Give a Mouse a Cookie*.) On your easel, display a sheet of chart paper with a sketch of your story idea. You will then explain how to plan the sentence you will write to go with your picture, and then write the sentence one word at a time.

> Today I am going to begin a story about going to the zoo. I have already drawn a quick picture to show you my story. Now I'm going to write the first sentence of my story. But first, I'm going to think about the story we have just read. In that story, certain things happened in order. First, the boy gave the mouse a cookie. Then, the mouse asked for a glass of milk. It went on and on in a certain order.
>
> I'm going to show you how we can plan a sentence in a certain order. This will help get us thinking about what we want to say, and it will help us remember the words we will write, so our sentence will make sense.

First, I will say my sentence out loud. **Second**, I will say each word of the sentence out loud and I will put up one finger for each word I say. **Third**, I will count the number of fingers that are up. **Fourth**, I will say the sentence again, matching my words to my fingers. **Fifth**, I will say the first word slowly, stretching it out. I will listen to the sounds that I hear in the word and I will write down the letter for each sound. When I don't hear any more sounds in the word, I will start on the next word. **Sixth**, I will read my sentence again. **Finally**, I will stop my sentence by putting a punctuation mark at the end.

I would like you to watch and listen as I write my first sentence.

(Say your sentence, and follow the above steps to write it down.)

Would you help me write just one more sentence?

(Say your second sentence, then have children work with you following the above steps to write the sentence.)

Let's think about the steps we followed to write this sentence. We'll make a chart to show the steps, so each of you can remember what to do when you are writing during Writer's Workshop.

(Create a chart with children and post it in the classroom. You may also want to create individual charts for them to keep in their writing folders; see right.)

A Plan for Writing

1. Say your sentence out loud.

2. Put up one finger for each word.

3. Count the fingers that are up.

4. Say the sentence again, matching the words to your fingers.

5. Say the words one at a time and write them.

6. Reread your sentence.

7. Stop your sentence with punctuation.

Connection:

Remind children that they can plan their writing and write each word for their sentence just as you did.

▪ Today when you write, try doing what we have done today and say your sentence, then follow the steps on the target chart to write your sentence.

(Call children one table at a time to get paper and go to their seats to work.)

Conference with children while they are working.

Reflection:

Consider this mini-lesson. What worked and what didn't? What would you do differently next year?

_____

_____

_____

_____

Mini-Lesson 34:
Spacing Is Important

Materials:
* Book that models the theme of crowding, such as *Too Many Frogs*, by Sandy Asher, or *Ten in the Bed*, by Penny Dale
* Markers

* Two sheets of chart paper: one with a picture you've sketched, along with a two- or three-sentence story *lacking* spaces between the words; the other sheet blank

Objective:
To teach children how important it is to leave space between words

Introduction:
Congratulate children on using A Plan for Writing. Then introduce the idea of spacing between words.

> ■ Boys and girls, I have noticed that many of you are using A Plan for Writing when you write. It really helps you to think about your sentence one word at a time so that you can write down the letters for the sounds you hear in each and every word in the sentence. Today we're going to think about the space we leave between words.

Instruction:
Read the story you selected, and then display your sketch and accompanying story, written without spaces.

> ■ Boys and girls, I would like you to help me read the story that I have written.
>
> (Read the story haltingly with the children's assistance.)
>
> We seemed to have some trouble reading my story. I wonder what could be wrong.
>
> (Some of the children will realize that you did not leave space between words.)
>
> Spacing between words seems to be important. Just as it wasn't good to be crowded in the story we read, it isn't good for words to be crowded either. I wonder if I could make it easier to read my story by writing it with spaces between each word.
>
> (Rewrite the story on a clean sheet of chart paper. You may want to follow A Plan for Writing if your children need that reinforcement.)
>
> Let's see. My first sentence is _____. I will say the first word and write down the letter for each sound that I hear. When I don't

hear any more sounds for that word, I cannot write any more letters for that word. I will stop that word, and then I will put a space. Then I will begin the next word.

(Continue until all of the words of the sentence are written with obvious spaces between each word.)

Now, let's see if it is easier to read my sentence.

Practice:

Allow children the opportunity to help you add another sentence to your story.

▪ Would you help me write just one more sentence? When we don't hear any more sounds for a word, would you hold your hand up like this (hand in a fist with pointer finger pointing up) so I will know to leave a space?

(Say your second sentence, encouraging children to indicate when spacing is needed.)

Let's remember this special signal for leaving a space. When we are writing like this, you will hold your pointer finger up in the air to show that we need to leave a space.

Connection:

Remind children that they can plan their writing and write each word, then leave a space for their sentence, just as you did.

▪ Today when you write, try doing what we have done today and leave a space after the word you have written so that you have spaces between all of your words.

Conference with children while they are working.

Reflection:

Consider this mini-lesson. What worked and what didn't? What would you do differently next year?

_____

_____

_____

_____

Mini-Lesson 35:
Seeing Spaces Between Our Fingers

Materials:
* Sheet of chart paper   * Markers

Objective:

To give children more practice on leaving space between words

Introduction:

Congratulate children on spacing between words.

■ Boys and girls, I noticed that you have been doing a great job remembering to put spaces between words when you write. That makes it so much easier for everyone to read what you have written.

Instruction:

Place a large sheet of chart paper on your easel.

■ Boys and girls, I am going to begin a new story today. The last time we met we had trouble reading my story and had to rewrite it putting spaces between the words. This time, I am going to use my hand to help me remember to add spaces. First, I will say my sentence out loud.

(Say your sentence, making sure it is no longer than five words.)

I will say my sentence again and put up a finger for each word I say. Now, look at my fingers.

(Be sure they are spread apart.)

Do you notice what is between my fingers? That's right, there are spaces between my fingers. Each of my fingers is a word I will write, and each space between my fingers is like the space I will leave between my words as I write them. Now, watch as I write my sentence.

(Write the sentence one word at a time with spaces between, referring to your fingers and spaces between them as you write.)

Spacing between words is important.

Practice:

Allow children the opportunity to help you add a second sentence to your story.

■ Would you help me write just one more sentence? When we don't hear any more sounds for a word, would you hold your hand up like this (hand in a fist with pointer finger pointing up) so I will know to leave a space?

(Say your second sentence, and ask children to hold up a finger for each word.)

With your other hand that you won't use for the space signal, would you put my sentence on your fingers being sure to spread your fingers apart so we will remember spaces?

(Have children help you remember spacing as you write the second sentence, one word at a time. Remind them to check their fingers for words and for spaces.)

Connection:

Remind children that they can use their hands to help them remember to space.

> Today when you write, try using your hands the way we have done today and leave a space after each word you write so that you have spaces between all of your words.

Conference with children while they are working.

Reflection:

Consider this mini-lesson. What worked and what didn't? What would you do differently next year?

_____

_____

_____

_____

Mini-Lesson 36:
Using Word Walls

Materials:
* Book that models the use of words in your writing, such as *The Boy Who Loved Words*, by Ron Schotter; *Max's Words*, by Byron Barton, or *First Thousand Words in English*, by Heather Amery

* Word wall
* Index cards and markers

Objective:

To show children how to use a word wall when writing

Introduction:

Congratulate children on the good work they are doing leaving spaces between words. Tell them that today, you're going to give them a new tool they can use when they write.

> Boys and girls, I noticed that so many of you are putting spaces between the words you write. It is making your sentences so much easier to read! Today we're going to use the word wall, to help us spell words when we write.

Instruction:

If you haven't already, point out to children your classroom word wall. Then introduce the book about words that you've selected.

■ Boys and girls, I have a book to read to you that tells about a boy who loves words. We are going to talk about words today.

(Read the book you've selected.)

You have learned how to plan your writing and how to leave space between words. Today we are going to talk about words and something you can use to help you write them down correctly on your papers. The tool is our word wall. Today I will teach you how we can add new words to our word wall and how we can use our word wall to help us spell words we want to write.

One word that we have been using a lot in our writing that we some-times have trouble spelling is the word _____. I will write that word on a card and we will put the card on the word wall under the letter that is at the beginning of our word. I will add the word _____ to the word wall under the letter __ since the word begins with that letter.

When I am writing, if I want to know how to spell that word, all I have to do is look at the word wall, find the letter that begins the word I want to spell, then look below that letter for the word I need. This is a tool to help us when we write.

Practice:

Have children work with you to add one or two more words to the word wall.

■ Another word that we might like to have on the word wall because we use it a lot is _____. Help me add this word to our word wall.

(Work with children to add a couple more words.)

Connection:

Remind children that they can use the word wall to help them spell words they want to write.

■ Today if you want to write one of the words we have added to our word wall and you don't know how to spell it, you can look right at the word wall to help you.

(Call children one table at a time to get their paper and go to their seats to work.)

Conference with children while they are working.

Reflection:

Consider this mini-lesson. What worked and what didn't? What would you do differently next year?

_____

_____

_____

_____

Mini-Lesson 37:
Using Mini-Offices to Help Us Write

Materials:
* Book that models the theme of going to the office, such as *Frida's Office Day*, by Thomas P. Lewis or *Lyle at the Office*, by Bernard Waber
* Mini-offices, prepared in advance, one per child (see instructions below)

Objective:
To show children how to use the mini-office as a writing tool

Introduction:
Congratulate children on using the word wall. Then introduce the mini-office tool.

> Boys and girls, I saw many of you looking at the word wall last time you were writing. It is a great tool to use when you're writing. Today, I'm going to give you a new tool called a "mini-office." This mini-office will be a place for you to keep word lists that will help you as you write.

MINI-OFFICE

To create the mini-offices, follow the steps below. Then laminate them, so they can be used year after year.

1. Glue or tape together two file folders, as shown, so there are three sections.

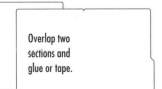

Overlap two sections and glue or tape.

2. Fold along the three seams to create a tri-fold.

3. Attach the following items to pages of the mini-offices: individual word wall, classmates' names (with pictures, if possible), color words, number words, and list of months and days. (These lists will be introduced in mini-lessons 38 to 42.)

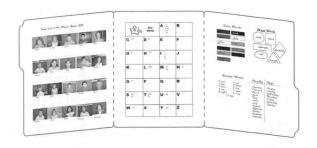

* Mini-offices can include a variety of useful aids. Here are some suggestions:
  • Individual word walls
  • Class list with names (and pictures)
  • Color words
  • Number words
  • Days and months
  • Shape names
  • ABC list

Instruction:

Read aloud the book you selected to introduce the concept of an "office." After a brief discussion, give each child his or her own mini-office.

> Boys and girls, the last time we met I taught you how to use a word wall. Today I am going to show you another tool to help you write. This is one that you will keep with your writing folder. It is called a mini-office. You can use this to collect some of your writing tools. It will be like your own private office.
>
> (Point out the various elements of the mini-office that you have handed out. You will explore these lists in greater depth in the next few lessons.)

Practice:

Encourage children to explore the features of the mini-office with their partners.

> Look at your mini-office to see what is on it. Turn to your partner and tell your partner one way your mini-office might help you when you write.
>
> (Allow time for partners to discuss, and then signal them to stop and look at you. Call on a few of the children to share their ideas.)

Connection:

Remind children that they will keep their mini-offices with their writing folders and that you will talk more about them over the next few days.

> Today you may use your mini-offices in the ways you have discovered. Remember, you will keep your mini-office with your writing folder. It will be your job to take care of it and to keep it nice.
>
> (Call children one table at a time to get their paper and go to their seats to work.)

Conference with children while they are working.

Reflection:

Consider this mini-lesson. What worked and what didn't? What would you do differently next year?

_____

_____

_____

_____

_____

Mini-Lesson 38:

Using Individual Word Walls to Help With High-Frequency Words

Materials:
* Individual word walls, contained in mini-offices
* Pencils or fine-point permanent markers

Objective:
To show children how to use the individual word wall in their mini-offices

Introduction:
The mini-offices contain several components that children will find handy as they're writing. Today, you'll introduce them to the individual word walls.

> Boys and girls, I saw many of you looking at the word wall last time you were writing. It is a great writing tool that you can use. Today, I want you to notice that you each have your very own word wall contained in your mini-office. This can help you spell some of the words you need when you're writing.

Instruction:
The individual word walls should include the words listed on your classroom word wall. Point these words out to children. Then tell them that in the future they can add more words to their word walls.

> Boys and girls, in your mini-offices you now have your very own word wall. I have filled in some words for you to help you when you're writing. When we want to add new words to our individual word walls, we can do it like this.
>
> (Demonstrate by adding words to a sample mini-office.)

Practice:
Have children add high-frequency words to their word walls—based on whatever criterion you choose. If the mini-offices are laminated, have children write with fine-point permanent markers. As you add additional words to the class word wall throughout the year, encourage children to add these words to their mini-office word walls.

Connection:
Remind children that they will keep their mini-offices with their writing folders and encourage them to use some of the words from their word wall in their writing today.

> Today you can use the word wall in your mini-office to help you write. Be sure to use some of the words from the word wall in your writing today.
>
> (Call the children a table at a time to get their paper and go to their seats to work.)

Conference with children while they are working.

Reflection:

Consider this mini-lesson. What worked and what didn't? What would you do differently next year?

_____

_____

_____

_____

Mini-Lesson 39:
Writing Our Classmates' Names

Materials:

* Book that models the use of names, such as *Chrysanthemum*, by Kevin Henkes; *The Name Jar*, by Yangsook Choi, *My Name Is Yoon*, by Helen Recorvits or *A Porcupine Named Fluffy*, by Helen Lester

* Class lists, contained in mini-offices

Objective:

To give children practice writing their classmates' names, and to help them to use their mini-office as a writing tool

Introduction:

Congratulate children on using the word wall in their mini-offices, and tell them today they are going to practice writing their classmates' names.

> Boys and girls, I saw many of you using your mini-offices last time you were writing. It is a great writing tool for us to use. Today we are going to use it to help us write classmates' names.

Instruction:

Read a book about names. For this lesson, we use *Chrysanthemum*, but any book that highlights names is fine. Discuss the importance of names, and how important it is to spell names correctly. Point out to children the class list contained in their mini-offices, which they can refer to when writing.

> Boys and girls, today we are going to read *Chrysanthemum*.
>
> (Read the book and discuss it briefly.)
>
> Just as Chrysanthemum's name was important, your classmates' names are important too. Everyone wants to have his or her name spelled correctly. Something that will help you do this is a list of your classmates' names.

> If I wanted to spell Kayla's name, I could look at my list and find it. Then I could see how to spell Kayla's, name and I could write it down, like this.
>
> (Demonstrate writing a couple of names.)

Practice:

Have each child find classmates' names on their own class list.

> Now you know how to use this list of your classmates' names. You can use it when you want to include someone's name in your writing. This is one more way we can use our mini-offices when we write.

Connection:

Remind children to use their lists today when they're writing.

> Today when you are writing, you will have your class list to use if you want to write someone's name. Remember that this list is always available in your mini-office. It will be your job to take care of it and to keep it nice.

Conference with children while they are working.

Reflection:

Consider this mini-lesson. What worked and what didn't? What would you do differently next year?

_____

_____

_____

_____

Mini-Lesson 40:
Writing Color Words

Materials:
* Book about colors, such as *My Many Colored Days*, by Dr. Seuss, or *A Color of His Own*, by Leo Lionni
* Lists of color names, contained in mini-offices

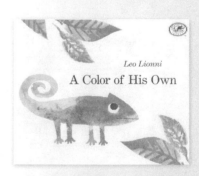

Objective:

To give children practice writing color words, and to help them to use their mini-office as a writing tool

Introduction:

Congratulate children on using the tools in their mini-offices, and tell them that today they are going to practice writing color words.

> ▪ Boys and girls, I saw many of you using your mini-offices last time you were writing. Some of you were using it to write the names of your friends. Today we are going to use it to help us write color words.

Instruction:

Read the book you selected, and use it as a springboard to discuss colors and how important they are. Point out that children will definitely want to write about colors, so knowing how to spell them will come in handy. Direct them to the list of color words in their mini-offices.

> ▪ Boys and girls, sometimes we want to write a color name but don't know how to spell it. This list of color names will help. If I wanted to spell *green*, I could look at my list and find it. Then I could see how to spell *green*, and I could write it down, like this.
>
> (Demonstrate writing a couple of color words.)

Practice:

Have each child find color names on their own list.

> ▪ Turn to your partner and tell him or her a color word you would like to spell. Your partner will find that word on his or her list and spell it for you. Take turns.
>
> Now you know how to use this list of color names. This is another way we can use our mini-offices when we write.

Connection:

Remind children to use their lists today when they're writing.

> ▪ Today when you are writing, you will have your list of color words to use when you write. Remember, that this list is always available in your mini-office. It will be your job to take care of it and to keep it nice.
>
> (Call the children one table at a time to get their paper and go to their seats to work.)

Conference with children while they are working.

Reflection:

Consider this mini-lesson. What worked and what didn't? What would you do differently next year?

_____

_____

_____

_____

Mini-Lesson 41:
Writing Number Words

Materials:
* Book that models the use of number words, such as *One Fish, Two Fish, Red Fish, Blue Fish*, or *Ten Apples Up On Top*, both by Dr. Seuss
* Number-word lists, contained in mini-offices

Objective:
To give children practice writing number words, and to help them to use their mini-office as a writing tool

Introduction:
Congratulate children on using the tools in their mini-offices, and tell them today they are going to practice writing number words.

> Boys and girls, I saw many of you using your mini-office last time you were writing. Some of you were using it to write the names of your friends and some of you were writing color names. Today we are going to use it to help us write number words.

Instruction:
Read a book with number words, and have a discussion about the importance of numbers. Point out to children the list of number words in their mini-offices.

> Boys and girls, sometimes we want to write a number word but don't know how to spell it. This list will help.
>
> If I wanted to spell *five*, I could look at my list and find it. Then I could see how to spell *five*, and I could write it down, like this.
>
> (Demonstrate writing a couple of number words.)

Practice:
Have each child find number words on their own list.

> Turn to your partner and tell him or her a number word you would like to spell. Your partner will find that word on his or her list and spell it for you. Take turns.
>
> Now you know how to use this list of number words. This is another way we can use our mini-offices when we write.

Connection:
Remind children to use their lists today when they're writing.

> Today when you are writing, you will have your list of number words to use when you write. Remember that this list is always available in your mini-office. It will be your job to take care of it and to keep it nice.

> (Call the children a table at a time to get their paper and go to their seats to work.)

Conference with children while they are working.

Reflection:

Consider this mini-lesson. What worked and what didn't? What would you do differently next year?

_____

_____

_____

_____

Mini-Lesson 42:
Writing Months and Days

Materials:
* Book that models the days of the week or months of the year, such as *Today Is Monday*, by Eric Carle
* List of days and months, contained in mini-offices

Objective:
To give children practice writing days and months, and to help them use their mini-office as a writing tool

Introduction:
Congratulate children on using the tools in their mini-offices and tell them today they are going to practice writing the names of months and days.

> Boys and girls, I saw many of you using your mini-office last time you were writing. Some of you were using it to write the names of your friends, and some of you were using it to write color and number words. Today we are going to use it to help us write the months and the days of the week.

Instruction:
Read a book that contains the names of the days or months. (You might want to repeat this lesson, first introducing days, then introducing months.) Point out to children the list of these words contained in their mini-offices.

> Writers, sometimes we want to write a day of the week or a month of the year but don't know how to spell it. This list will help.
>
> If I wanted to spell *Monday*, I could look at my list and find it. Then I could see how to spell *Monday*, and I could write it down, like this.
>
> (Demonstrate writing a couple of words.)

Practice:

Have children find words for the days of the week or the months of the year on their own list.

> Turn to your partner and tell him or her a day or month you would like to spell. Your partner will find that word of his or her list and spell it for you. Take turns.
>
> Now you know how to use this list of months and days. This is one more way we can use our mini-offices when we write.

Connection:

Remind children to use their lists today when they're writing.

> Today when you are writing, you will have your list of months and days to use when you write. Remember, that this list is always available in your mini-office. It will be your job to take care of it and to keep it nice.
>
> (Call the children a table at a time to get their paper and go to their seats to work.)

Conference with children while they are working.

Reflection:

Consider this mini-lesson. What worked and what didn't? What would you do differently next year?

_____

_____

_____

_____

Mini-Lesson 43:
Using Rubber Bands to Help Us Spell

Materials:
* Book that models stretching, such as   * Rubber band
  Noodle, by Munro Leaf

Objective:

To teach children to stretch out words when spelling

Introduction:

Review how much children have already learned about writing. Then introduce the day's lesson.

■ Boys and girls, you have already learned a lot about writing this year. Today I am going to teach you some ways to stretch out words you don't know when you are writing.

Instruction:
Read the book you've selected, then discuss it and relate it to stretching words using rubber bands. For this lesson, we use *Noodle,* by Mumro Leaf.

■ Writers, the dog in this book is a dachshund. Dachshunds are little dogs that look like they have been stretched out. This makes me think of something else that stretches. Rubber bands stretch. Sometimes when I want to write a word and don't know how to spell it, I stretch it out and listen for all of the sounds in the word, and then I write the letters for the sounds I hear.

(Hold up a rubber band.)

When I stretch out a word, I think of a rubber band. As I say the word slowly, I stretch it out, the way a rubber band stretches out.

(Demonstrate stretching two or three words, stretching out the rubber band as you say the word. Then set the rubber band aside, and tell children that you often just pretend the rubber band is there. You can still stretch out words. Demonstrate with a couple more words.)

Practice:
Have each child pretend to hold a rubber band between their hands and stretch it out as they stretch out words, listening for the sounds and saying what letters stand for those sounds.

■ Listen carefully to the word I say. Now, stretch the word out with me. Listen for the sounds you hear in the word. What letters stand for those sounds?

(Write words on chart paper as children stretch out the word and volunteer letters for the sounds they hear.)

Connection:
Ask students to try rubber-banding when writing.

■ When you don't know how to spell a word, you can pretend you're holding a rubber band in your hands. Stretch it out as you stretch out the word, and listen carefully for the sounds you hear. Then write down the letters for those sounds. This is a tool to help you write words you don't know how to spell.

(Call children one table at a time to get their paper and go to their seats to work.)

Conference with children while they are working.

Reflection:
Consider this mini-lesson. What worked and what didn't? What would you do differently next year?

_____

_____

_____

_____

Mini-Lesson 44:
Using Arm Spelling to Help Us Spell

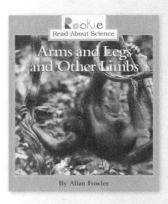

Materials:
* Book that models the use of your arms and legs, such as *Arms and Legs and Other Limbs*, by Allan Fowler

Objective:
To give children practice stretching out words when spelling

Introduction:
Congratulate children for using rubber-band spelling. Then introduce the day's lesson.

> Boys and girls, I noticed several of you rubber-banding words you did not know how to spell. Today I am going to teach you another way to stretch out words you don't know when you are writing: arm spelling.

Instruction:
If possible, read *Arms and Legs and Other Limbs*, by Allan Fowler, and discuss it. Then relate it to stretching words using your arms.

> Boys and girls, today we are going to read the book *Arms and Legs and Other Limbs,* by Allan Fowler.
>
> (Read the book and discuss it briefly.)
>
> We can use our arms to help us stretch out words. First I will say the word. Then I will say it slowly putting my right hand to my left shoulder and saying the beginning sounds for the word, then I will move my hand down to my elbow and say the middle sounds for the word, and finally I will move my hand down to my wrist and say the ending sounds for the word. Then I will move my right hand all the way down my left arm, from the shoulder to the wrist, and blend all of the sounds together and say the whole word.

> ■ Sometimes when I want to write a word and don't know how to spell it, I use my arm and I stretch the word out and listen for all of the sounds in the word, and then I write the letters for the sounds I hear. You can do the same thing.

Practice:

Have each child practice using his or her arm to stretch out words, listening for the sounds and telling what letters stand for those sounds. Write the words on chart paper as children stretch out the word and volunteer letters for the sounds they hear.

Connection:

Ask students to try stretching out word using their arm while they are writing.

> ■ When you don't know how to spell a word, you can stretch out the word using your arm, and listen carefully for the sounds you hear. Then write down the letters for those sounds. This is a way to help you write words you don't know how to spell.
>
> (Call children a table at a time to get their paper and go to their seats to work.)

Conference with children while they are working.

Reflection:

Consider this mini-lesson. What worked and what didn't? What would you do differently next year?

_____

_____

_____

_____

UNIT 7: TELLING STORIES

The mini-lessons in this unit are all about telling stories. Most children are natural oral storytellers, yet when it comes to writing, those same students can find themselves at a loss when facing a blank sheet of paper. The lessons that follow will help you show children that they have a lot to write about, whether by drawing on their own lives and experiences, or by calling on their imaginations. We also include lessons that encourage children to tell a story without words, and to marry words and illustrations, just as their favorite picture book authors do.

Mini-Lesson 45:
We All Have Stories to Tell
(You can repeat this lesson, using different books.)

Materials:
* Book that models stories from our own lives, such as *Tell Me a Story, Mama*, by Angela Johnson, *If You Were a Writer*, by Joan Lowery Nixon, or *Cherries and Cherry Pits*, by Vera B. Williams

Objective:
To help children find stories from their own lives

Introduction:
Point out to children that we all have stories to share and that we enjoy sharing our stories.

> ■ Has your mother or father ever told you a story? Have you ever told someone else a story? We all have stories to share, and it is fun to share our stories. What kinds of stories might you be able to share with us, with your family, or with your friends? When I ask you to, turn to your partner, knee to knee, and tell your partner what kinds of stories you might share.
>
> (Allow a few minutes for discussion, and then call on a few volunteers to share what their partners told them.)

Instruction:
Read the book you've selected and then have a discussion about it, leading children to the conclusion that we all have stories to share.

> ■ We all have stories. Every day we have stories we can share. Some of you may even have stories about your school day that you share when you get home.

Practice:

Have children work with their partners to think of kinds of stories to share.

> There are all kinds of stories that you might want to share. You might share stories about sports games, your school day, a birthday party, what you did on a vacation, a ride in a car, a day at the park, a new pet, or a brother or sister. I know you love to tell stories because many of you come into the classroom in the morning ready to tell me or your classmates a story.

Connection:

Remind children that there are all kinds of possible stories to share.

> Today at your desks, see if you can draw and write one of the stories you have to share.

Conference with children while they are working.

Share Time:

Gather children together for share time and ask one child to share how he or she told a story today in writing. Have children turn to their partners and share.

Reflection:

Consider this mini-lesson. What worked and what didn't? What would you do differently next year?

_____

_____

_____

_____

Mini-Lesson 46:

Discovering Treasures That Are Near and Dear to Our Hearts

Materials:

* Book that models finding a treasure, such as *The Treasure*, by Uri Shulevitz

* Paper sack and instruction heart (see sidebar on page 89)

Objective:

To help children identify topics that are "near and dear to their heart"

Introduction:

Introduce the idea that something we treasure is "near and dear to our hearts."

> Yesterday we talked about how fun it is to share stories. But you may be wondering how you will decide what stories to write. Today I am going to teach you that you can tell stories about things that are "near and dear to your heart."

Instruction:

Read *The Treasure*, if possible, or another book you've selected. Then discuss the story and help children reach the conclusion that a treasure is something that is near and dear to our hearts.

> A treasure is something that is worth a lot to a person. We all have things that mean a lot to us, things we treasure, just like in the story.

Practice:

Help students understand that something they treasure is "near and dear to their hearts."

> Today I'm going to give everyone a special bag. When you go home, I want you to find something that you treasure and put it in the bag. Tomorrow, you will bring your bag to school and you will share your treasure.

Connection:

Continue to discuss the idea that something you treasure is something that is near and dear to your heart.

> Boys and girls, what does it mean when we say "near and dear to my heart"?
>
> (Allow a couple of minutes for discussion.)
>
> Something that is near and dear to my heart is something that is very important to me; it is something that I treasure. Today, when you go back to your seats to write, think about things you treasure.
>
> (Send children back to their seats to draw and write.)

Conference with children while they are working.

Reflection:

Consider this mini-lesson. What worked and what didn't? What would you do differently next year?

_____

_____

_____

_____

Instructions for Take-Home Sack

Create a special take-home bag for each child to transport his or her treasured object to school.

Use any small bag (paper lunch bags work well) and attach instructions in a heart-shaped cutout, so parents can help children if needed. The heart-shaped cutout should read:

Find something at home to put into this bag — something you treasure, something that is near and dear to your heart. We will write about our treasures tomorrow.

Glue heart-shaped cutout to the front of a paper bag as shown.

Mini-Lesson 47:
We Tell Stories About Things We Love

Materials:
* Your heart box or bag with treasure inside
* Children's bags, with treasure from home inside
* Chart paper
* Marker

Objective:
Students will identify topics that are "near and dear to their hearts"

Introduction:
Tell students that today they will share their treasures and then write about things that they love.

> Yesterday you took home a paper sack and filled it with a special treasure. I know that you found something near and dear to your heart because many of you have been very eager to share what you brought. First, I will share my treasure with you.

Instruction:
Model how to write a piece about something that is near and dear to your heart. First, reveal your treasure and explain why the item is near and dear to your heart. Then, on a sheet of chart paper, quickly write a brief piece about your treasure.

> Now I will write about my treasure. I will tell about the person who gave it to me and why the item is near and dear to my heart.

Practice:
Give children time to share the treasures they brought in their bags.

> You have brought something that is near and dear to your heart, something that is very important to you and that you treasure.

Call on a few children to share. If time is limited, have only a couple share, then have children turn to their partners to share their treasures.

Connection:
Tell children that something near and dear to their heart makes a good subject to write about.

> I wrote about my treasure today, and now you will write about your treasure. Today, I when you go back to your seats, I would like you to write about the item inside your heart bag. It is something near and dear to your own heart.

Conference with children while they're working.

Share Time:
When the students have gathered together for share time, ask one student to read his or her writing to the rest of the class. Ask students to share with their partner what they wrote.

Reflection:
Consider this mini-lesson. What worked and what didn't? What would you do differently next year?

_____

_____

_____

_____

Mini-Lesson 48:
We Tell Stories About Things We Have Done

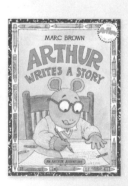

Materials:
* Book featuring a character who writes about something in his or her life, such as *Arthur Writes a Story*, by Marc Brown

Objective:
To help children identify things that they have done in their lives, which they can write about

Introduction:
Introduce the idea to children that their personal experiences make great writing topics.

> ▪ Writers, lately we have been writing about what is near and dear to our hearts. Today we will discover that there are lots of things that we have done, and we can write about these things, too.

Instruction:
Read your selected book. (For this lesson, we use *Arthur Writes a Story*.)

> ▪ As I read *Arthur Writes a Story*, by Marc Brown, think about how Arthur came up with the story he needs to write for school.

Practice:
Lead a discussion about how Arthur came up with his story idea.

Connection:
Have students turn to their partner to share something that has happened in their lives that they could write about today during Writer's Workshop.

> After listening to *Arthur Writes a Story*, by Marc Brown, you learned how Arthur came up with a story to write about for school. You have just talked with your partner about something that has happened in your life that you can write about also. Today during Writer's Workshop I want you to write about something that has happened to you.

Conference with children while they are working.

Share Time:
Gather children together for share time and ask one student to read his or her writing to the rest of the class. Then ask children to share with their partner what they wrote about today.

Reflection:
Consider this mini-lesson. What worked and what didn't? What would you do differently next year?

_____

_____

_____

_____

Mini-Lesson 49:
We Tell Stories About Things We Have Seen

Materials:
* Chart paper
* Marker

Objective:
To help children identify things that they have seen in their lives, which they can write about

Introduction:
Introduce the idea that things children have seen in their lives can be great topics to write about.

Instruction:

Model how to think of something you have seen and then write about it.

> ■ Last time, we wrote about something we have done. Today I want you to think about something that you have seen in your life that you can write about. I am going to think of something that I have seen that I can write about. Let me think; I have seen a lot in my life so far.
>
> (Model aloud your thinking, so children can see and hear what it looks like.)
>
> I know what I can write about. This summer my family and I went on vacation to the ocean. I want to write about what I saw when we went to the beach. I am going to do a quick sketch of the beach we visited, and then I will add words to go with it.
>
> (As you do a quick sketch, make sure you think aloud as you draw it.)
>
> After drawing I will add words to my sketch.

Practice:

Lead a discussion about how you came up with something you'd seen, and how you sketched a drawing and then added words to it. Tell children that they will follow these steps today when they write.

Connection:

Have students turn to their partner to share something that they have seen that they can write about today.

> ■ I want you to sit knee to knee with your partner and take turns talking about something you have seen that you could write a story about.

Give students about two or three minutes to share with their partner what they have seen and how they are going to write about today during Writer's Workshop.

Conference with children while they are working.

Share Time:

Gather children together and ask a volunteer to read his or her writing to the rest of the class. Ask students to share with their partner what they wrote.

Reflection:

Consider this mini-lesson. What worked and what didn't? What would you do differently next year?

_____

_____

_____

_____

Mini-Lesson 50:
We Can Tell Stories Using Our Imaginations

Materials:
* Book that models storytelling, such as *The Stories Julian Tells*, by Ann Cameron

Objective:
To show children that they can tell stories about anything, even if it is made up

Introduction:
To start, point out to children that sometimes when we write, we use our imaginations.

> In the last few days you have learned that you can tell stories about what is "near and dear" to you. And you can tell stories about things you have done and things you have seen. Sometimes we can make up stories using our imaginations. These stories can be wild and crazy or funny or mysterious.

Instruction:
Read a chapter from *The Stories Julian Tells*, or another book you've selected. Explain that Julian likes to tell stories.

> Julian used his words to tell this story. Just like Julian did, you can make up a good story using your imagination.

Practice:
Have students turn to their partner and tell a make-believe story to their partner.

> Now use your imagination to think of something you could tell a story about. Please turn to your partner to share.

Connection:
Remind children that there are all kinds of possible stories to share.

> We have learned that people tell stories out loud. You have told a story using your words to your partner. Now, you are going to remember the story you told and write it down on paper using pictures and written words.

Conference with children while they are working.

Share Time:
Gather students together for share time and ask one student to read the story he or she wrote. Have students turn to their partners and take turns sharing their stories.

Reflection:

Consider this mini-lesson. What worked and what didn't? What would you do differently next year?

_____

_____

_____

_____

_____

Mini-Lesson 51:
We Use Pictures to Tell Stories

Materials:
* An assortment of wordless books, such as those by Mercer Mayer

Objective:
To show children that stories can be told using pictures

Introduction:
Tell children that sometimes people tell stories without using words. They use pictures alone. Show some examples.

> ▪ We've been learning about all the different ways that we can tell stories. We've learned that everyone has stories to share and that they enjoy sharing them. Today we will see that sometimes we can tell stories without using any words.

Instruction:
Show students the books you've selected.

> ▪ We read wordless books by looking at the pictures carefully and making up the story in our heads based on what the pictures are showing. Today we're going to read these wordless books in small groups.

Practice:
Have students read a wordless book in a small group, and then discuss together what the book was about.

> ▪ Today I'm going to have you go back to your tables. I will give each table a wordless book. Read your book together, and then we will gather again as a group and talk about the books you have read.

Connection:

After discussing the books, remind children that their stories may be told using pictures alone.

> ■ Just like these authors, you can share your stories using just pictures.
> Today, I want you to tell a story using only pictures and no words.

Conference with children while they are working.

Share Time:

Gather children together for share time, and ask one student to share how they told their story today using pictures. Have students turn to their partners and share.

> ■ When I ask you to turn to your partner, you will turn knee to knee and you will show your partner your paper and tell your partner your story. Your partner will listen carefully. You will take turns.

Reflection:

Consider this mini-lesson. What worked and what didn't? What would you do differently next year?

_____

_____

_____

_____

_____

Mini-Lesson 52:
Sometimes Our Stories Are Hard to Draw

Materials:
* Book that models doing your best, such as *Ish*, by Peter H. Reynolds
* Chart paper
* Marker

Objective:
To show students that what's important is doing their best, and to keep going

Introduction:
Tell students that sometimes you see them hesitate to draw particular topics because they aren't sure how to draw the subject. Tell them you'll show them what you do in that case.

▪ Writers, I have been very excited about the kinds of things that you have been talking and writing about. But sometimes I see you excited about a great idea, and then you go back to your seats and you're not sure how to draw the picture you have in mind. And some of you actually decide not to write about your great idea because you aren't sure how to draw it! That is so sad because the world missed out on your wonderful idea. Today I want to show you what I do when I have the "Oh, no" feeling.

Instruction:

Read the book *Ish* or another book you've selected. Then model a writing situation in which you encounter difficulty, consider options for an easier topic, and then decide to persist with the challenging subject.

▪ I'm going to do a piece of writing, and partway through it, you'll see me get that "Oh, no, I don't know how to draw it!" feeling. I want you to be researchers and watch what I do when I get that feeling.

Okay, I want to tell the story of the time I had an ice cream and then rode on the roller coaster.

(Proceed to tell your story and draw to illustrate it. Then, midway through, stop.)

Oh, no! Oh, no! I don't know how to show the roller coaster. Forget it; I'll just draw a sunny day and flowers. I know how to draw flowers.

(Pause dramatically and shake your head. Then say, aloud, but to yourself.)

No, no, wait a second. Should I stop? Or should I just keep going and draw the best I can?

Practice:

Ask your students what to do next. Have them first tell their partner and then tell you what to do next. Follow their advice.

▪ Boys and girls, would you tell the person beside you what I could do now. Should I give up and draw flowers?

(Allow children a few seconds, and then ask one for advice. Be sure to choose a child who will tell you to do the best you can.)

Really? Do the best I can and go on? That's what writers do? Yes, writers do the best they can and keep going!

(Draw quickly to finish the illustration.)

Connection:

Ask students to name what they saw you doing when you got to the tricky part of the drawing. Remind them that you expect they will draw their own pictures the best way they can.

So writers, I'm hoping that today, if you get to a tricky part of your picture, you will do what I did and just draw it the best you can and not give up!

Conference with children while they are working.

Share Time:

Gather children together for share time, and ask one student to share how they told their story today in their writing. Have students turn to their partners and share.

Reflection:

Consider this mini-lesson. What worked and what didn't? What would you do differently next year?

_____

_____

_____

_____

_____

Mini-Lesson 53:

We Use Pictures and Words to Tell Stories, Just Like Our Favorite Authors Do

Materials:
* A book children are familiar with, one that has a picture on each page coupled with a sentence or two, such as *Corduroy*, by Don Freeman

Objective:

To give students practice drawing and writing, using their favorite picture book authors as inspiration

Introduction:

Remind students that their favorite authors put words and pictures together on the page. Today they will practice doing just what their favorite authors do.

Writers, during our Writer's Workshop, each of you has thought of things you do and things you care about. You held those in your mind and then put them on the page. And I can look at your pictures and your stories and learn real details about your life, which is so exciting! Today you are going to practice telling a story with pictures and words, just as your favorite authors do.

Instruction:

Display the book you've selected. For this lesson, we use *Corduroy*.

- Do you all remember this book?

    (Hold up the book for children to see.)

    You can see that the author, Don Freeman, used pictures and words to tell this story. Where are the pictures? Where are the words? The author used pictures and words to tell his story. I am telling you this because you can do something similar to what Don Freeman did. You can write pictures on the top of your pages and words on the bottom of your pages.

Practice:

Give children paper and ask them to point on their pages to the place where they will draw and the place where they will write.

- Look at your writing paper. Everyone point to the place where you will draw your picture. Everyone point to where you are going to put your words.

Connection:

Remind children to use pictures and words.

- So writers, today I am hoping that each of you will use pictures and words to tell your story.

Conference with children while they are working.

Share Time:

Gather children together for share time and tell them that you are very pleased that you saw lots of details in their drawings today. Ask one or two students to share how they told their story today in their writing. Have students turn to their partners and share.

Reflection:

Consider this mini-lesson. What worked and what didn't? What would you do differently next year?

_____

_____

_____

_____

_____

UNIT 8: USING PUNCTUATION

Punctuation is crucial to writing sentences that mean what we want them to. In the four mini-lessons in this unit, you'll introduce students to the three end-punctuation marks: the period, the question mark, and the exclamation point. You'll help children practice using these marks in their own writing to ensure that when they write, their meaning is clear. Lessons can be repeated as needed.

Mini-Lesson 54:
We Use Periods at the End of Telling Sentences

Materials:
* A Big Book to model the use of periods as ending punctuation, such as *Miss Mary Mack*, by Mary Ann Hoberman, *The Napping House*, Audrey Wood, or *Pumpkin Pumpkin*, by Jeanne Titherington (If possible, choose a book that contains periods only, without other end punctuation.)

* Highlighting tape
* Chart paper
* Marker

Objective:
To teach students when to add a period at the end of a sentence

Introduction:
Students will understand that they need to end a telling sentence with a period.

> Many of you are beginning to write stories that are longer than one sentence. Today we are going to talk about how to use punctuation marks to stop our sentences. This will make your stories easier to read.

Instruction:
Explain to students that punctuation is a very important part of writing. Then tell them that every telling sentence ends with a period.

> Writers, we've read this book before, and we're going to read it together today and as we do so, we're going to be "punctuation detectives."
>
> (Choral read the book. Then turn to each page of the book, one page at a time, and asking students to find the end punctuation.)
>
> Who can find the punctuation mark that comes at the end of the sentence?
>
> Great, that is a punctuation mark! What is its name?
>
> (After periods are identified, highlight them with highlighting tape.)
>
> What do periods do? Yes, they stop a telling sentence.

Practice:

Begin to create a Punctuation Marks anchor chart, which you will add to over the next two lessons.

Draw a period and then illustrate its use with a sample sentence, such as "Our class likes to read."

Punctuation Marks	
● period	Our class likes to read.

Connection:

Tell the students that they will use a period to stop their sentence when it is a telling sentence.

> Today and from now on, when you are writing a telling sentence you will end it with a period.

Conference with children while they are working.

Share Time:

When the students have gathered together for share time, ask one student to share how he or she used a period to stop a telling sentence. Have students turn to their partners and share how they used a period at the end of their sentences.

Reflection:

Consider this mini-lesson. What worked and what didn't? What would you do differently next year?

_____

_____

_____

_____

Mini-Lesson 55:
We Use Question Marks at the End of Questions

Materials:

* A big book to model the use of question marks as ending punctuation, such as *Is Your Mama a Llama?*, by Deborah Guarino, or *The Little Mouse, the Red Ripe Strawberry, and the Big Hungry Bear*, by Don and Audrey Wood (Be sure to choose a book that has lots of question marks.)

* Punctuation Marks anchor chart
* Marker
* Highlighting tape

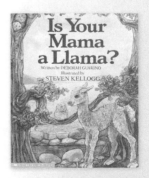

Objective:

To teach students they must add a question mark at the end of an asking sentence

Introduction:

Remind students that punctuation is very important. Explain to students that whenever a sentence is asking a question it should end with a question mark.

> ▪ Yesterday we learned that writers use punctuation marks so that their stories are easier to read. We learned that you use a period when you write a telling sentence. Today we are going to learn when you use a question mark at the end of a sentence.

Instruction:

Explain that the punctuation mark you are going to teach them about today is the question mark. Read the book you've selected.

> ▪ Writers, we've read this book before, and we're going to read it together today and as we do so, we're going to be "punctuation detectives."
>
> (Choral-read the book. Then turn to each page of the book, one page at a time, and asking students to find the end punctuation.)
>
> Who can find the punctuation mark that comes at the end of the asking sentence?
>
> Great! What is the name of this punctuation mark?
>
> (After question marks are identified, highlight them with highlighting tape.)
>
> What do question marks do? Yes, they stop an asking sentence.

Punctuation Marks	
● period	Our class likes to read.
? question mark	Do you like books?

Practice:

Add the question mark to your Punctuation Marks anchor chart. Draw a question mark and then illustrate its use with a sample question, such as "Do you like books?"

> ▪ Let's add the question mark to our punctuation chart.

Connection:

Tell the students that they will use a question mark to stop their sentence when it is an asking sentence.

> ▪ Today and from now on, when you are writing an asking sentence you will end it with a question mark. Be sure to include at least one question mark in your writing today.

Conference with children while they are working.

Share Time:

Gather students together for share time and ask one or two students to share how they used a question mark to stop their asking sentences. Then have students turn to their partner and share how they used a question mark in their writing.

Reflection:

Consider this mini-lesson. What worked and what didn't? What would you do differently next year?

_____

_____

_____

_____

Mini-Lesson 56:
We Use Exclamation Points to Show Excitement

Materials:
* A big book to model the use of exclamation points as ending punctuation, such as *No, David!*, by David Shannon, or *I Like Me!*, by Nancy Carlson (Be sure to choose a book with lots of exclamation points.)

* Punctuation Marks anchor chart
* Marker
* Highlighting tape

Objective:

To teach students when to add an exclamation point at the end of a sentence

Introduction:

Remind students that punctuation is very important. Explain to children that they should use an exclamation point to end a sentence that shows excitement.

> Boys and girls, we have learned that writers use punctuation marks so that their stories are easier to read. So far, we have learned to use periods after telling sentences. And we learned to use question marks after asking sentences. Today we are going to learn what punctuation mark to use at the end of a sentence to show excitement.

Instruction:

Read the book you've selected.

> Writers, we've read this book before, and we're going to read it together today and we're going to be "punctuation detectives."
>
> > (Choral read the book. Then turn to each page of the book that has an exclamation point and ask students to find the end punctuation.)

> Who can find the punctuation mark that comes at the end of the sentence? Great! What is the name of this punctuation mark?
>
> (After the exclamation points are identified, highlight them with highlighting tape.)
>
> What do exclamation points do? Yes, they stop an "emotion" or "excitement" sentence.

Punctuation Marks		
•	period	Our class likes to read.
?	question mark	Do you like books?
!	exclamation mark	Look out!

Practice:

Add the exclamation mark to your Punctuation Marks anchor chart. Then add a sample sentence to illustrate its use—for example, "Look out!"

> Now we'll add the exclamation point to our Punctuation Marks chart.

Connection:

Tell the students that they will use an exclamation point to stop their sentences when they show emotion or excitement.

> Today and from now on, when you are writing a sentence with emotion you will end it with an exclamation mark. Be sure to include at least one exclamation point in your writing today.

Conference with children while they are working.

Share Time:

Gather children together for share time and ask one or two children to read their writing to the rest of the class and share how they used exclamation points. Then ask children to share with their partner how they used an exclamation mark to stop their sentences that show emotion or excitement.

Reflection:

Consider this mini-lesson. What worked and what didn't? What would you do differently next year?

_____

_____

_____

_____

Mini-Lesson 57:
We Always Use Punctuation to Stop Our Sentences

Materials:
* A book about punctuation, such *Punctuation Pals*, by Dr. Hope, *Perfect Pop-Up Punctuation Book*, by Kate Petty, or *Punctuation Takes a Vacation*, by Robin Pulver

* Punctuation Marks anchor chart

Objective:

To reinforce the idea that writers must always use punctuation marks to end their sentences

Introduction:

Again, remind children that punctuation is very important. Tell children that whenever they write they need to end a sentence in one of three ways: with a period, with a question mark, or with an exclamation point.

> The last few days we have learned that writers use punctuation marks so that their writing is easier to read. We also learned that there are three sentence stoppers and we learned what they look like and when to use them.

Instruction:

Explain that today children are going to learn how the three types of end punctuation can all work together. First review the Punctuation Marks chart, then read the book you've selected.

> Punctuation marks are a lot like signs you see on the roads. Punctuation marks are very important. Who can remember the names of these punctuation marks?
>
> (Point to the Punctuation anchor chart and have children say the names of the punctuation marks with you.)
>
> Great, I am glad you remembered those names. Keep them in mind as I read.

Practice:

Talk about the different sentence stoppers and their purpose. Have the students give you examples of sentences for each punctuation mark.

Connection:

Tell the students that they will use punctuation marks to stop their sentences when they write.

> Today and every day when you are writing, you will use punctuation marks to stop your sentences. You will use either a period, a question mark, or an exclamation point at the end of each sentence you write.

Conference with children while they are working.

Share Time:

Gather students together for share time, and ask one student to read his or her writing to the rest of the class.

> Today I saw many good authors using punctuation marks at the end of their sentences.

Ask students to share with their partner the kinds of punctuation marks they used at the end of their sentences.

Reflection:

Consider this mini-lesson. What worked and what didn't? What would you do differently next year?

_____

_____

_____

_____

_____

Unit 9: Making Our Writing Even Better

Revision is a fundamental aspect of writing. As students become more and more proficient with print, their ability to revise will grow stronger. But even at this early stage, it's important to help children understand that writers seldom "get it right" the first time around, and that going back and "fixing things up" is an essential step in the process—and one they will never outgrow. The mini-lessons in this unit will introduce a Fix It Up! chart and checklist to help students make their writing the best it can be.

Mini-Lesson 58:
We Can Make Our Writing Better by Fixing It Up

Materials:
* Book about fixing things, such as *Fix It, Sam*, by Lori Ries, or *Fix-It Duck*, by Jez Alborough
* Story written on chart paper, containing several errors
* Marker

Objective:
To show children that their writing can be made better by fixing it up (an introduction to revising and editing)

Introduction:
Congratulate children on the wonderful work they have been doing, and introduce the concept of revising or "fixing up" writing.

> When we write, we don't always get it right the first time. That's the way it is for everybody. Today we're going to learn how to make our writing even better! We're going to learn that anytime we write, we can go back and fix up things that need fixing.

Instruction:
Place a story you've written that contains several mistakes on your easel. Read the book you've selected, and point out that writers fix things, too.

> Today I am going to teach you how you can make your writing even better by fixing things up. Sometimes we need to know how to fix things, just like the character in the book we read.

> When I write, I always go back and read what I have written to see if there is anything I need to fix. I always try to make my writing better. I have just finished writing a story. Now I need to fix it up. Look at my story with me as I fix the first part.

(Read the first paragraph and make corrections, thinking aloud as you find mistakes and reason to yourself what needs to be done to fix them.)

Practice:

Ask children to help you fix up the rest of your story.

■ Would you help me find anything I need to fix in the next part of my story?

(As children volunteer, have them locate the mistakes and then explain what to do to fix up the writing and tell why it needs to be done.)

Connection:

Remind children that they can fix up their own writing to make it better.

■ Today, after you write, go back and read what you have written. Look for anything that you can fix to make your writing better.

(Call children one table at a time to get paper and go to their seats to work.)

Conference with children while they are working.

Reflection:

Consider this mini-lesson. What worked and what didn't? What would you do differently next year?

_____

_____

_____

_____

_____

Mini-Lesson 59:

We Can Make Sure Our Words Match Our Pictures

Materials:

* Any picture book with text under picture (preferably a Big Book)
* Marker
* Chart paper

* A selection of picture books with coordinated text and illustrations, one book for each student pair

Objective:

To reinforce the idea that pictures and text should match when writing a story

Introduction:

Tell children what a good job they did fixing up their writing last time you met. Tell them that today they're going to make sure their words and pictures match.

> ■ I noticed that many of you really worked hard to fix up your writing last time we had Writer's Workshop. One way you can do this is to make sure your words and pictures go together.

Instruction:

Read the book you've selected, and point out that the words and text go together.

> ■ Today we are going to look at some books to see how the picture and the words match on each page.
>
> (Show a few books, noting the matching illustrations and text.)

Practice:

Ask partners to look at a book together to see if the pictures match the words. (Use books at or below their reading levels.)

> ■ I am going to give partners a book to look at together. First look at the picture. Then look at the words. Decide together if the picture matches the words.
>
> (Give a book to each pair. Allow a few minutes for the children to look through the books. When most are finished, signal them to stop.)
>
> How many of you had books with pictures that matched the words? You all did! Authors know that pictures and words should match. When they write books they make sure that the pictures show what the words tell about.

Connection:

Remind children that they can make their pictures and words match. On a sheet of chart paper, create a Fix It Up! chart that you will add to over several lessons.

> ■ Today, when you write and draw, be sure to check that your pictures show what your words tell. This is something we do to make our writing better.
>
> We're going to make a Fix It Up! chart to help us remember to fix up our writing. Today, we'll begin the chart with the reminder to make sure our words and pictures match.
>
> (Begin chart by writing: "Do your pictures and words match?" Then call children a table at a time to get paper and go to their seats to work.)

Fix It Up!

1. cat

Do your pictures and words match?

Conference with children while they are working.

Reflection:
Consider this mini-lesson. What worked and what didn't? What would you do differently next year?

_____

_____

_____

_____

Mini-Lesson 60:

We Can Make Sure Our Sentences Start With Uppercase Letters

Materials:
* Any Big Book
* Story you've written on chart paper, containing several capitalization errors
* Highlighting tape
* Fix It Up! chart

Objective:
To teach children that they should capitalize the first word of a sentence

Introduction:
Tell children what a good job they did fixing up their writing during the last Writer's Workshop. Then introduce the day's lesson.

> I noticed that many of you really worked hard last time to make sure your pictures matched your writing. You did just what our Fix It Up! chart reminds us to do. Today we're going to learn that every sentence starts with an uppercase letter.

Instruction:
Use a big book and highlighting tape to demonstrate that each sentence begins with an uppercase letter.

> Today we are going to look at a Big Book to see if each sentence begins with an uppercase letter. Let's use highlighting tape make the uppercase letters really stand out.
>
> (Use the Big Book to highlight a few uppercase letters at the beginning of sentences.)

Practice:
Show children a story that you have written. It should contain several capitalization errors.

■ Writers, I would like for you to help me with a story I have written. I haven't fixed it up yet, and I think there may be some mistakes. Let's look to see if I have used uppercase letters at the beginnings of each of my sentences.

(Call on volunteers to "fix up" your writing by drawing a line through the lowercase letters you have written at the beginning of your sentences and writing the uppercase letters above them.)

Connection:

Remind children that they can fix up their writing by making sure they have used a uppercase letter at the beginning of each sentence.

■ Today, when you write and draw, you will make sure your pictures show what your words tell. Then you will check to be sure each sentence begins with an uppercase letter.

We're going to remember that this is important by adding it to our Fix It Up! chart.

(Add "Does every sentence begin with an uppercase letter?" to the chart. Then call children one table at a time to get paper and go to their seats to work.)

Conference with children while they are working.

Fix It Up!
1. → cat Do your pictures and words match?
2. <u>A</u> cat is a pet. Does every sentence begin with an uppercase letter?

Reflection:

Consider this mini-lesson. What worked and what didn't? What would you do differently next year?

_____

_____

_____

_____

_____

Mini-Lesson 61:
We Can X Out Words to Fix Them

Materials:
* Story written on chart paper, containing a number of words that have missing letters (e.g., *dg* for *dog* and *fst* for *fast*)
* Marker
* Fix It Up! chart

Objective:

To show children that they can cross out words and make corrections

Introduction:

Tell children how much you have been enjoying their stories and what a great job they are doing. Then introduce the day's lesson.

> ▪ Wow, boys and girls. I've noticed that you have really been working on fixing up your writing. Today we're going to talk about what to do when you find you have spelled a word incorrectly.

Instruction:

Use the story you've written on chart paper to demonstrate how to cross out an error.

> ▪ Boys and girls, you know that when we write, we stretch the word out like a rubber band and we write down every sound we hear. Today I am going to show you what to do if you have already written your story and you go back to read it and you find out you have not stretched a word out.
>
> I have a story that I have already written, but I haven't fixed it yet. I'd like you to help me see if there are any words I could stretch out better, so that there is a letter for each sound we hear.
>
> (As children notice words that could be better, X them out, and work together to stretch the word out, then write a letter for each sound. Do this with a couple of the words.)

Practice:

Have children practice crossing out words that have not been stretched out and writing the corrected word above.

> ▪ Now that you know how to X out a word and write the stretched-out word above, I'm going to call for a volunteer to help with the next word we find that needs to be fixed.
>
> (Have children fix more of the words in the same manner.)

Connection:

Remind children that they can fix up their writing by X-ing out words that have not been stretched out and then writing the corrected version above.

> ▪ After you have written your story today, be sure to read it and look to see if you need to fix anything. Remember our Fix It Up! chart. Does your picture match your words? Do all of your sentences begin with a capital letter? Do you see any words that have not been stretched out? If you do, then X them out and write the stretched-out word above.
>
> Today we will add this to our Fix It Up! chart to remind us that we can X out a word and fix it by writing the correct word above the old one.

Fix It Up!
1.  → cat
Do your pictures and words match?
2. <u>A</u> cat is a pet.
Does every sentence begin with an uppercase letter?
3.   X
Have you X-ed out words that need to be fixed?

(Add "Have you X-ed out words that need to be fixed?" to the chart. Then call children a table at a time to get paper and go to their seats to work.)

Conference with children while they are working.

Reflection:

Consider this mini-lesson. What worked and what didn't? What would you do differently next year?

_____

_____

_____

_____

Mini-Lesson 62:
We Can Add Words We Forgot

Materials:
* A story you've written on chart paper, with several words left out
* Marker
* Fix It Up! chart

Objective:
To show children that they can add words they left out by using a caret

Introduction:
Tell children how much you have been enjoying their stories and what a great job they are doing. And introduce the day's lesson.

> ■ Writers, I've noticed that you have really been working hard to make your writing even better. You have been doing just what our Fix It Up! chart reminds us to do. Today we're going to talk about what to do when you leave out a word in a sentence.
>
> (Briefly review chart.)

Instruction:
Use your story to demonstrate how to insert a word that has been left out of a sentence.

> ■ Today I am going to show you what to do when you read the story you have written and discover that you have left out a word.

(As you read the first part of your story, children will notice that words are missing. Show them how to make a caret [∧], and then add the missing word.)

This little symbol is called a "caret." It's looks like a little arrow, and it points to the spot where we want our word to go.

Practice:

Have children practice inserting the missing words by using a caret.

- Now I want you to help me check to see if more words are missing. As I read more of the story, if you notice a word is missing, put your fingertips together to make a caret. I will notice your hands and will stop reading. Then I will ask one of you to help me put the caret and the word in where they should be.

  (As children listen and determine where to place the carets and words, have volunteers write them in.)

Fix It Up!
1.  **cat** Do your pictures and words match?
2. <u>A</u> cat is a pet. Does every sentence begin with an uppercase letter?
3. **X** Have you X-ed out words that need to be fixed?
4. **∧** Have I added any words that are missing?

Connection:

Remind children that they can fix up their writing by making sure they have not left out words, and if they have, by using a caret to add the word or words they left out.

- After you have written today, be sure to read it and look to see if you need to fix anything. Remember our Fix It Up! chart. Does your picture match your words? Do all of your sentences begin with a capital letter? If you find words that have not been stretched out, have you X-ed them out and written the stretched-out word above? Are any words missing? Today we will add a new step to our Fix It Up! chart. It will remind us that if we need to add a word, we can add the word by using a caret.

  (Write: "Have I added any words that were missing?" to the chart. Then call children one table at a time to get paper and go to their seats to work.)

Conference with children while they are working.

Reflection:

Consider this mini-lesson. What worked and what didn't? What would you do differently next year?

_____

_____

_____

_____

Mini-Lesson 63:
We Make Sure Our Sentences End With Punctuation

Materials:
- * A story you've written on chart paper, with end punctuation missing
- * Marker
- * Fix It Up! chart

Objective:
To teach children to check for punctuation at the end of sentences

Introduction:
Tell children how much you have been enjoying their stories and what a great job they are doing. Then introduce the day's lesson.

> ▪ Boys and girls, I've noticed that you have really been working hard to make your writing even better. The last time we met, you learned how to add words when you leave them out of your story. You have been doing just what our Fix It Up! chart reminds us to do. (Briefly review chart.) Today we're going to learn to check for punctuation at the end of sentences.

Instruction:
Use the story you've written to demonstrate for students how to check for punctuation marks at the end of sentences and add them when needed.

> ▪ We know that when we finish a piece of writing we always want to go back and check to see if we can make it better. Today I'm going to show you what to do when you read the story you have written and find out that you have left out a punctuation mark at the end of a sentence.
>
> (As you read the first part of the story, children will notice that punctuation marks are missing. Have them tell you where to add them, and what kind to add.)

Practice:
Have children practice adding missing punctuation.

> ▪ I want you to help me check to see if more punctuation marks are missing. As I read more of the story, if you notice a period, question mark, or exclamation point is missing, raise your hand. If a period is missing, make your hand into a fist. If a question mark is missing, curl your fingers. If an exclamation mark is missing, hold your fingers up straight. I will ask one of you to help me put in the correct punctuation mark.
>
> (As children listen and determine where to place the punctuation marks, have volunteers write them in.)

Fix It Up!
1.  → cat   Do your pictures and words match?
2. <u>A</u> cat is a pet.   Does every sentence begin with an uppercase letter?
3. X   Have you X-ed out words that need to be fixed?
4. ∧   Have I added words that are missing?
5. • ? !   Do all of my sentences end with a punctuation mark?

Connection:

Remind children that they can fix up their writing by making sure they have not left out punctuation marks, and if they have, by adding the correct punctuation mark.

> Boys and girls, when we finish a piece of writing we get to check it and make it even better! After you have written today, be sure to read it and look to see if you need to fix anything. Today we're going to add a new step to our Fix It Up! chart. We will add a period, question mark, and exclamation point to our Fix It Up! chart to remind us that every sentence must end with a punctuation mark.
>
> (Add "Do all of my sentences end with a punctuation mark?" to the chart. Then call children one table at a time to get paper and go to their seats to work.)

Conference with children while they are working.

Reflection:

Consider this mini-lesson. What worked and what didn't? What would you do differently next year?

_____

_____

_____

_____

Mini-Lesson 64:

We Reread Our Work Carefully and Use a Checklist to Help Edit Our Work

Materials:
* A story you've written on chart paper, with some errors
* Individual copies of the Fix It Up! Checklist
* Marker
* Fix It Up! chart (laminated before this lesson)

Objective:

To show children how to use an editing checklist when they write

Introduction:

Tell children how much you have been enjoying their writing and what a great job they are doing. And introduce the lesson.

> Boys and girls, I've noticed that you have really been working hard to make your writing even better. The last time we met, you learned

how to add words when you leave them out of your story. You have been doing just what our Fix It Up! chart reminds us to do.

(Briefly review chart.)

Today we're going to get a new tool to help us as we write: a checklist.

Instruction:

Together with students, use the Fix It Up! Checklist to check your story and correct errors.

■ Today I am going to show you how to use our Fix It Up! chart to help find mistakes in our writing. Before we start, I am going to change our chart into a checklist by adding a box in front of each sentence. Now our Fix It Up! chart is a Fix It Up! Checklist. Watch as I use this checklist to help me fix up my story for today.

(Read item one on the Fix It Up! Checklist and then check the teacher story to see if that item is correct. If so, check it off. Continue with a couple more items.)

Practice:

Have children practice using the checklist to fix up work.

■ I would like you to help me use the checklist to fix up the rest of my story. Let's look at the next item on the checklist. Help me see if I need to fix anything for this item.

(Make changes as children point them out. Then continue with additional items on the checklist. Be sure to just cover one checklist item at a time.)

Connection:

Remind children that every day they can fix up their writing and they can use a Fix It Up! Checklist to help them.

■ After you have written your story today, be sure to read it and look to see if you need to fix anything. Remember to use a Fix It Up! checklist. You can use this checklist every day when you write, to help you make your writing as good as it can be.

Call children one table at a time to get paper and a Fix It Up! Checklist and go to their seats to work.

Reflection:

Consider this mini-lesson. What worked and what didn't? What would you do differently next year?

✓	Fix It Up! Checklist
1. 🐱 —→ cat	Do your pictures and words match?
2. <u>A</u> cat is a pet.	Does every sentence begin with an uppercase letter?
3. X	Have you X-ed out words that need to be fixed?
4. ∧	Have I added words that are missing?
5. . ? !	Do all of my sentences end with a punctuation mark?

_____

_____

_____

_____

UNIT 10: WRITING FOR MANY PURPOSES

The mini-lessons in this unit introduce students to some of the many genres of writing, and the reasons we use them—and then encourage children to try to their hand at each. So they'll learn about lists and greeting cards, journal entries and poems. More than with the other units in this book, you may wish to carry out the lessons in Unit 10 on more than one day, starting the lesson one day, and continuing it the next. The written pieces that the lessons inspire can be as brief or as elaborate as you like. It all depends on you and your students, and your time constraints. But we guarantee that this unit will inspire some memorable student work!

Mini-Lesson 65:
We Write for Many Reasons

Materials:
> * Samples of several types of writing you have done—you may wish to include a list, a sign, a newsletter article, a greeting card, a how-to piece, an autobiographical piece, a diary entry, or a short personal narrative.

Objective:
> To introduce children to various types of writing

Introduction:
> Praise children for their efforts at "fixing up" their writing. Tell them that now that they are becoming more skilled writers, there are many types of writing they can do.

>> Boys and girls, authors write for many different reasons. Now that you are doing such a great job as writers, there are lots of different things you can write.

Instruction:
> Share with children some examples of different types of writing you have done, and briefly introduce different purposes for writing.

>> Today I am going to show you that authors write for many purposes. I write a lot each day for many different reasons. I have some of the things I have written here to share with you.
>>
>> (Briefly share each piece of writing and explain your reason for writing it.)

Practice:

Give children several different scenarios and ask them to tell their partner what kind of writing would probably be used for that situation.

> ■ We know that there are many reasons for writing, and we know that we would use a different type of writing for each different reason. We are going to practice thinking about what kind of writing would be best for different situations.
>
> > (Give different situations, and then have children turn to their partners to decide what type of writing would be most appropriate. For example, Ben is going to spend the weekend at Grandma's and wants to write down all the things he needs to take with him. Mia has had a great day and wants to remember it forever. Abby's mother is having a birthday. Noah is going to write a report about dinosaurs for his teacher.)

Connection:

Tell children to think about the kind of writing they are doing today. Remind them to use their Fix It Up! Checklist to help make their writing even better.

> ■ After you have finished your writing today, be sure to read what you have written and look to see if you need to fix anything. Remember to use a Fix It Up! Checklist to make your writing even better.
>
> > (Call children a table at a time to get their paper and go to their seats to work.)

Conference with children while they are working.

Reflection:

Consider this mini-lesson. What worked and what didn't? What would you do differently next year?

_____

_____

_____

_____

_____

Mini-Lesson 66:

We Can Make Signs and Posters

Materials:
* Samples of signs and posters
* Book about signs, such as *I Read Signs*, by Tana Hoban, *Signs at the Store*, by Mary Hill, or *The Sign on Rosie's Door*, by Maurice Sendak

* A variety of signs and posters
* Paper for making signs or posters

Objective:
To show children that signs and posters are a type of writing

Introduction:
Tell children what a good job they did last time identifying different kinds of writing. Explain that today they're going to learn about one kind of writing: posters and signs.

> Boys and girls, last time we met we talked about different kinds of writing. Today we are going to think about just one kind of writing. We are going to talk about making signs and posters.

Instruction:
Read the book you've selected to introduce signs. Share a couple of signs and describe their purposes.

> Last summer I had a garage sale and made this sign so that people would know what I had to sell and how to get to my house. I made this poster to let people know how fun it is to read.

Practice:
Show children several more signs and posters (or pictures of them, if you don't have enough actual signs) and have students identify which they are and what their purpose might be.

> We see signs and posters everywhere we go. I have some pictures of signs and posters. When I show you a picture, tell your partner whether it is a sign or a poster and why it was made.

Connection:
Tell children to think about making either a sign or a poster. Remind them to think of the purpose for making it before they start.

> Turn to your partner and tell your partner whether you are going to make a sign or a poster. Then tell your partner why you will make it and what it will say.
>
> > (Call children one table at a time to get their paper and go to their seats to work.)

Conference with children while they are working.

Share Time:

Gather students together for share time and ask one or two students to share their poster or sign. Have students turn to their partners and share. Then hang the children's finished signs and posters around the room.

Reflection:

Consider this mini-lesson. What worked and what didn't? What would you do differently next year?

_____

_____

_____

Mini-Lesson 67:
We Can Make Lists

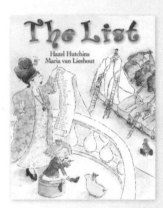

Materials:

* Book about lists, such as *The List*, by Hazel Hutchins, *Wallace's Lists*, by Barbara Bottner, or *The 10 Best Things About My Dad*, by Christine Loomis
* Samples of lists
* Chart paper
* Marker

Objective:

To teach children that a list is a type of writing, what a list looks like, and how to make one

Introduction:

Tell children what a good job they did last time with their posters and signs. If you have time, discuss two or three. Then explain that today they're going to learn about another kind of writing: a list.

> Boys and girls, you know that we write for many different purposes. Making posters and signs is one kind of writing we can do. Another kind of writing is a list.

Instruction:

Read the book you've selected to introduce lists. Discuss the kinds of lists the characters made, and share more examples of lists, explaining that we use lists to help us remember and keep track of things. Then, on a sheet of chart paper, demonstrate how you make a list.

> Today I need to make a list of things I need from the grocery store. If I make a list, I won't forget anything I need. First, I will make a title for my list: "My Shopping List." Next, I will think of the things I need to get. I will write number one, and then write the first thing: milk. Now, I will write number two, and then I will write the second

thing I need: bread. I will keep adding numbers and things I need until I am finished with my list. When I am finished I will put my list in a safe place so I will have it when I go to the grocery store. It will help me remember what I need.

Practice:

Have children volunteer titles for lists they could make. Write them on chart paper.

> ■ Remember that a list helps us remember something. Think of a list you might want to make. We will make a list of the titles you think of.

Connection:

Tell children to think about making a list that would help them remember something.

> ■ Turn to your partner and tell your partner what list you will make today. You may even want to use one of the titles on our list or you may want to think of a different one.
>
> (Call children one table at a time to get their paper and go to their seats to work.)

Conference with children while they are working.

Share Time:

Gather children together for share time and ask one or two students to share their lists. Have students turn to their partners and share their lists.

Reflection:

Consider this mini-lesson. What worked and what didn't? What would you do differently next year?

_____

_____

_____

Mini-Lesson 68:
We Can Make Greeting Cards

Materials:
* Samples of greeting cards
* A book about greeting cards, such as *Sophie and the Mother's Day Card*, by Kaye Umansky, *Happy Birthday, Good Knight*, by Shelley Moore Thomas, or *The Jolly Postman*, by Janet and Allan Ahlberg
* Large sheet of paper, folded to look like a greeting card
* Markers
* Construction paper for making cards (pre-folded)

Objective:

To teach children that a greeting card is a type of writing, what a greeting card looks like, and how to make one

Introduction:

Tell children what a great job they did with making lists. Then explain that today they're going to learn about another kind of writing: a greeting card.

> Boys and girls, you know that we write for many different purposes. Making posters and signs is one kind of writing we can do. Another kind of writing is a list. And another kind of writing we can do is a greeting card.

Instruction:

Read the book you've selected to introduce greeting cards. Discuss the kind of card the character in the story made. Then share examples of greeting cards, explaining that we use cards to let people know we care about them by remembering their birthday or some other important event. Then demonstrate how to create a greeting card.

> Today I want to make a birthday card for my daughter. I will make a pretty picture on the front and I will write "Happy Birthday!" at the top. I will leave the next page blank. Then I will write a short message wishing my daughter a happy birthday on the third page of the card. I will sign my name. Now, my card is ready to be given to my daughter.

Practice:

Give each child a blank card and have him or her tell what will be written or drawn on each page.

> Think of a card to make for someone you care about. Tell your partner what you will write or draw on each part of the card.
>
> (Allow time for children to tell their partners what they will write or draw.)

Connection:

Remind children that greeting cards are another type of writing and that we write for many purposes.

> We write for many reasons. Sometimes we make greeting cards for people we care about. When you go back to your desk, make a greeting card for someone special.
>
> (Call children one table at a time to go to their seats to work.)

Conference with children while they are working.

Share Time:

Gather children together for share time, and ask one or two students to share their greeting cards. Have students turn to their partners and share their greeting cards. Encourage children to deliver or send their cards to their intended recipients.

Reflection:

Consider this mini-lesson. What worked and what didn't? What would you do differently next year?

_____

_____

_____

_____

Mini-Lesson 69:

We Can Write Letters

Materials:

* Samples of letters
* A book about letters, such as *A Letter to Amy*, by Ezra Jack Keats, *Click, Clack, Moo: Cows That Type*, by Doreen Cronin, or *Dear Mr. Blueberry*, by Simon James

* Chart paper
* Markers
* Lined paper, for children's letters

Objective:

To teach children that a letter is a type of writing, what a letter looks like, and how to write one

Introduction:

Tell children what a great job they did making greeting cards. Then explain that today they're going to learn about another kind of writing: a letter.

> Writers, you know that we write for many different purposes. We can making posters and signs. We can make lists and greeting cards. Another kind of writing we can do is letter writing.

Instruction:

Read the book you've selected to introduce letter writing, and discuss. Then share some sample letters, explaining that we write letters to other people to tell them about ourselves and what we are doing. On a sheet of chart paper, demonstrate how to write a letter.

> Today I want to write a letter to my friend, Gail. Watch and listen as I show you how I will write my letter.
>
> (Think aloud as you compose and finish the letter.)

Practice:

Make a list of reasons to write a letter.

> Think of a reason you might send a letter to someone. Let's make a list of Reasons to Write a Letter.

(Create the list on chart paper as children volunteer reasons for letter writing. Possible reasons include to invite a friend over to play, to thank Grandma for a present, to tell a friend you haven't seen in a while what you have been doing.)

Connection:

Remind children that letters are another type of writing and that we write for many purposes. Tell children that today they will write a letter to someone they know.

> We write letters to let other people know about us or about things we are doing or to ask questions and find out about them. We made a list of reasons for letter writing. You might wish to use one of these reasons when you write today.
>
> (Call children one table at a time to get their paper and go to their seats to work.)

Conference with children while they are working. Encourage children to deliver or send their letters to their intended recipients.

Reflection:

Consider this mini-lesson. What worked and what didn't? What would you do differently next year?

_____

_____

_____

_____

Mini-Lesson 70
We Can Write a Newsletter or Newspaper Article

Materials:
* Samples of newspapers and newsletters
* A book about newspapers, such as *Coyote School News*, by Joan Sandin
* Chart paper
* Marker

Objective:

To show children that newspaper and newsletter articles are a type of writing, what an article looks like, and how to write a one

Introduction:

Tell children that today they will learn that newspaper and newsletter articles are another type of writing. This writing tells people the about latest news and events.

■ Today we are going to learn that newspapers and newsletters are another type of writing we can do.

Instruction:

Read *Coyote School News* or another book to introduce news writing to students, and discuss it. Then share examples of newspapers and newsletters, explaining that people write them to inform others about news, events, and important topics.

■ Today I want to write a newspaper article about bike riding in the city. More and more people are riding bikes in the city. It saves gas and it's good exercise. I think this is an interesting topic and that people would like to read about it. Watch and listen as I show you how I will write my news article.

(Think aloud as you complete the newsletter or newspaper article.)

Practice:

Make a list of reasons we would write a newsletter or newspaper article.

■ Think of a reason you might write a newsletter or newspaper article. Let's make a list of Reasons to Write a Newsletter and/or Newspaper article.

(Construct the list on chart paper as children volunteer reasons for writing a newsletter or newspaper article. Possible reasons for newsletter: to inform parents about what we are doing at school, to talk about special activities coming up or special dates. Reasons for writing a newspaper article: to inform the public about something, to report on a sporting activity, to share ideas about a topic of interest.)

Connection:

Remind children that newsletters and/or newspaper articles are another type of writing and that we write for many purposes.

■ We write newsletters and newspaper articles to let other people know about things we are doing, special activities, to inform the public about something, and report on a community activity. On the chart, we made a list of reasons for writing a newsletter and/or newspaper article. You might want to use one of these reasons when you write today.

(Call children one table at a time to get their paper and go to their seats to work.)

Conference with children while they are working.

Share Time:

Gather students together for share time and ask one or two students to share their news articles. Have students turn to their partners and share their writing.

Reflection:

Consider this mini-lesson. What worked and what didn't? What would you do differently next year?

_____

_____

_____

_____

Mini-Lesson 71
We Can Write Poetry

A VERY FIRST BOOK OF POETRY

Materials:
* Book of children's poetry, such as *The Random House Book of Poetry for Children*, by Jack Prelutsky, *Poetry for Young People*, by Langston Hughes, or *Here's a Little Poem*, by Jane Yolen

* Samples of poems
* Chart paper
* Marker

Objective:
To show children that poetry is a type of writing, and to have them write a free-verse poem

Introduction:
Tell children what a great job they did with writing their news articles. Remind them that there are so many different kinds of writing they can do. Explain that today they will learn another one: poetry.

Instruction:
Read some poems from the text you've selected to introduce poetry. First read some poems that rhyme, and discuss them. Then read a few free-verse poems—poems that don't follow a meter or have rhyme. Tell students that some poems rhyme, but not all poems do.

> Poets are able to see ordinary things in new and different ways. When they write, they make their words sound like music and we hear rhythm and rhyme in their words.
>
> I like to write free-verse poetry. The fun thing about free verse is that I can use colorful words, but I don't have to rhyme. I can also use punctuation in fun ways. I can break my words up and write my words in whatever way I wish to make my poem more meaningful. When we write poems, our lines don't have to go all the way to the right side of the page!

Practice:

Write a free-verse poem with the class. Free verse is an appropriate choice for young children, as it does not adhere to strict guidelines and children can easily experience success.

> I would like to write a free-verse poem, but I would like you to help me choose colorful words as I write.

Write a short poem about an ordinary thing, having students volunteer words. Talk about using colorful words, about the placement of words, and about the punctuation marks you might choose.

> Tiny, little, miniature bird
> with a needle-sharp beak
> pecking,
> Pecking,
> PECKING,
> in the soft black dirt.
> What have you found?
> A WIGGLY WORM!!

Connection:

Remind children that we write for many purposes and that we write poems because they're fun to write and fun to share.

> We write for many reasons. We write poems to tell our thoughts and feelings. We can look at ordinary things in different ways and we make our words sound like music. We play with words and we have fun with punctuation. We write poetry because it is fun. Today, you can write a poem about anything you choose.
>
> (Call children one table at a time to get their paper and go to their seats to work.)

Conference with children while they are working.

Share Time:

Gather students together for share time and ask one or two students to share the poems they wrote. Have students turn to their partners and share their poems.

Reflection:

Consider this mini-lesson. What worked and what didn't? What would you do differently next year?

_____

_____

_____

_____

Mini-Lesson 72
We Can Write in a Diary or Journal

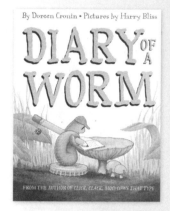

Materials:

* A book about diaries or journals, such as *My Prairie Summer*, by Sarah Glasscock, *Diary of a Wombat*, by Jackie French, or *Diary of a Worm*, by Doreen Cronin

* Journal for you to write in
* Journal for each child (spiral notebooks work well)

Objective:

To show children that diary entries are a type of writing, and to have them complete the first entry in a journal

Introduction:

Tell children what a great job they did with writing poetry. Then introduce the day's lesson.

> Boys and girls, I was excited to read your free-verse poems. You used so many colorful words. I could tell you had a lot of fun writing your poems. Today I'm going to tell you about another kind of writing you can do: journal writing.

Instruction:

Read the book you've selected to introduce diaries. Then model writing a diary or journal entry, thinking aloud.

> Boys and girls, we write in a diary or journal to remember things that have happened in our lives. Sometimes, we don't share what we wrote with anyone. It's just for us. But we can share it if we want to.
>
> I am going to write about what happened to me this morning. I don't want to forget it, so I'm going to write it down. I am going to use this book to write in. It is a book with empty pages. Each day I will write on a new page and I will tell about things that happened to me that day. I will always begin by writing the date. That way, I will always remember when things happened. This book will be my journal. Watch as I write today's date and write my first entry.

Practice:

Give each children their own journal to write in each day. Have them tell their partners what they will write today.

> Turn to your partner and tell him or her what you are going to write in your journal today.

Connection:

Remind children that journals are another type of writing they can do.

We write in diaries and journals to tell about things that have happened to us. That way we will never forget them. We can share what we write if want to, but sometimes the writing is just for us.

(Call children one table at a time to go to their seats to work. Decide beforehand if you want these to be response journals, or not. If you choose to write responses to the children's entries, let children know where to put the journals when they are finished.)

Conference with children while they are working.

Reflection:

Consider this mini-lesson. What worked and what didn't? What would you do differently next year?

_____

_____

_____

_____

Mini-Lesson 73
We Can Write Autobiographies With Lots of Details

Materials:
* Personal narratives, such as *A Chair for My Mother*, by Vera B. Williams, *Owl Moon*, Jane Yolen, or *The Paperboy*, by Dav Pilkey

* Chart paper
* Marker

Objective:
To have children write a personal narrative, paying attention to details

Introduction:
Tell children what a great job they have been doing. Then introduce the day's lesson.

Boys and girls, you've been doing a wonderful job writing in your journals. Today we're going to learn about another type of writing we can do: autobiography.

Instruction:
Read the story you've selected and discuss it, focusing on the use of details. At this point, writing about themselves won't be a new idea for children, but

take this opportunity to introduce the word *autobiography*, and tell students that what makes autobiography—and most writing—really vivid and exciting is adding juicy details.

> ■ Writers, you know that you can tell stories about yourself and your life. When we do this, we are writing autobiography. That word means a story about our life. Some authors write stories about their whole lives, and some authors write about just one part, or one thing that happened to them. Some authors, like this one, do a great job of telling about a little thing that has happened and they add details about how things look, or how they sound, or how they feel, or even how they smell or taste. They really use their senses to add a lot of interesting details to their stories. This helps the readers to make pictures in their mind.

Practice:

Have children recall details from the story. Allow students time to share with partners. Then have several children share their partners' responses and write them on a sheet of chart paper.

> ■ I would like you to think of details that you heard in the story I just read. Turn to your partner to share one thing that really made a picture in your brain.

Connection:

Remind children to add details to make their stories more interesting.

> ■ When you write today, think about something that has happened to you, then add details that will help me make pictures in my brain when I read your story.
>
> (Call children one table at a time to get their paper and go to their seats to work.)

Conference with children while they are working.

Share Time:

Gather students together for share time and ask one or two students to share the personal narratives they wrote. Have students turn to their partners and share their pieces.

Reflection:

Consider this mini-lesson. What worked and what didn't? What would you do differently next year?

_____

_____

_____

_____

Mini-Lesson 74
We Can Gather Information Before Writing

Detail Sheet

<u>Frogs</u>
Topic

1. _____
2. _____
3. _____
4. _____
5. _____

Materials:
* Nonfiction book, such as *Frogs*, *Dinosaurs*, or *Monarch Butterfly*, all by Gail Gibbons
* Chart paper
* A tub of nonfiction books from which students may select
* Markers
* Detail sheet for each student

Objective:
To help children identify important details in a nonfiction book

Introduction:
Tell children that as a class you have been reading and discussing many nonfiction books. Point out that many nonfiction books feature lots of details that give us information.

> Boys and girls, we've been reading and talking about a lot of nonfiction books. Today, we are going to read a book called *Frogs* by Gail Gibbons. As you listen, notice the details she shares to help us learn about frogs.

Instruction:
Read *Frogs*, or another book you've selected. After each main idea, stop and discuss the information found in the book and identify the important details on those pages. Then continue reading and discussing, and have children pull out important details as you read. (If you have a Big Book, use highlighting tape to identify the details located.)

Practice:
Have children work with partners. Have them decide together on two to three important details; then, on chart paper (or an enlarged detail sheet) write down five important details children volunteer.

> Turn to your partner and talk about the important details that you noticed in the book we read together. Then decide an important detail from this book. When I give the signal, we will stop talking and I will ask you to share.

Connection:
Have partners choose a book from the nonfiction tub. (These books should have been previously read to children so they are already familiar with them.) Give each child a detail sheet and have them together identify five important details from the book they have selected.

> When you are working with your partner today, find five important details from the book you have selected, and write them down on the detail sheet. (Younger children may need to draw pictures.)

Share Time:
Gather students together for share time and ask one or two students to share the important details they found. Have students turn to their partners to share the information they discovered.

Reflection:
Consider this mini-lesson. What worked and what didn't? What would you do differently next year?

_____

_____

_____

_____

Mini-Lesson 75
We Can Write an Informational Piece

Materials:
* Nonfiction book chosen from previous lesson (Students will also need the book they selected in the previous lesson.)
* Group detail sheet created in previous lesson
* Chart paper
* Marker
* Students' detail sheets created in previous lesson

Objective:
To have children write an informational nonfiction piece

Introduction:
Tell children that as a class you have been find important details in nonfiction books. Now you're going to take those details and write an informational

Instruction:
Show the group detail sheet that was created for the previous lesson. Demonstrate how to turn the details into sentences to create a nonfiction piece. For example, if "lay eggs" is listed on your sheet, show children how to write this as a sentence: "Frogs lay eggs." Then continue creating sentences with each detail to create a complete nonfiction piece.

Practice:
Have children think about an important detail they discovered the day before. Ask a few volunteers to turn their detail into a sentence and share it aloud. Then have the other students turn to their partners and share their sentence.

■ Think of an important detail that you listed on your detail sheet.
With your partner, share this detail in a sentence.

Connection:

Have children work with a partner to write sentences (two or three for kindergarten, more for more advanced writers) using information they gathered in the previous lesson from the nonfiction book they selected.

■ Boys and girls, you are going to work with your partner to write sentences just like you shared together. You will write sentences about the important details you gathered from your nonfiction book to write an informational piece.

Share Time:

Gather children for share time, having them bring their sentences. Allow time for two or three children to share.

Reflection:

Consider this mini-lesson. What worked and what didn't? What would you do differently next year?

_____

_____

_____

_____

Writing Conferences
What are they? What do they look like? What do they sound like?

The writing conference is the heart of Writer's Workshop. The writing conference lets you engage in a mode of teaching that most of us imagined when we entered this profession—one-on-one interaction with students. When a writing conference works well it can have real benefit for the student. You talk with a student, dialogue about his or her writing, make suggestions, and then move on. Most teachers discover that conferencing with a student feels natural. But don't be surprised if you feel a little uncomfortable at first. If your experience was like ours, most of the teachers we had assigned, corrected, and graded our writing. We never experienced the kind of writing conference that is being described here.

Fortunately, conferencing is a skill we can all learn. Here are some conferencing fundamentals to keep in mind as you begin conferring one-on-one with your students.

Be a Good Listener

We all know what it means to be a good listener, but putting it into practice is harder than it sounds. Writer's Workshop challenges the idea of the paradigm "Teachers talk and students listen." During a conference children must be active participants, not passive recipients. This requires that you be a responsive listener.

Be Attentive as a Reader

Try to react to student writing as you would respond to any other piece of writing you enjoy reading. Laugh if it is funny. If it's sad, make sure the student knows you feel the sadness in it. Let the child see that his or her writing has affected you. Show interest!

Understand the Writer

In a conference you are attempting to get a handle on what the child is doing (or trying to do) in his or her writing. Draw on the knowledge of the student's history as a writer. Once you understand his or her goal, your job is to scaffold to help the child achieve it. Patience is key. No skill is acquired overnight, but with steady practice, students will make real strides.

Build on the Student's Strengths

Writers tend to be fragile and highly sensitive. Give concrete praise during the first part of a writing conference. Often we as teachers are better at finding errors and weaknesses in a piece of writing than locating and congratulating children on the parts that are working well. When you give students specific praise and single out their effort, they are more open to taking risks and trying new things.

Choose One Teaching Point

Pick one teaching point as the focus of your conference, even though there may be many issues to choose from. Lucy Calkins says, "Teach the writer, not the writing." The idea is to add to the young writer's knowledge of strategies—not merely to improve a particular piece of writing. Our goal as teachers is to improve all the writing that the students will do.

Book List for Primary Mini-Lessons for Writer's Workshop

Unit 1: Basic Routines

- *Harold and the Purple Crayon* by Crockett Johnson, HarperCollins, 1998 (Lesson 3)
- *My Crayons Talk* by Patricia Hubbard, Henry Holt, 1999 (Lesson 3)
- *Look! Look! Look!* by Nancy Elizabeth Wallace, Marshall Cavendish, 2006 (Lesson 4)
- *Communication* by Aliki, Greenwillow Books, 1999 (Lesson 4)
- *Listen and Learn* by Cheri Meiners, Free Spirit, 2003 (Lesson 5)
- *Can You See What I See?* by Walter Wick, Cartwheel, 2002 (Lesson 5)
- *Can I Help?* by Marilyn Janovitz, North-South Books, 1998 (Lesson 6)

Unit 2: Getting Started

- *Nana Upstairs & Nana Downstairs* by Tomie dePaola, Putnam, 2000 (Lesson 8)
- *Thunder Cake* by Patricia Polacco, Putnam, 1997 (Lesson 8)
- *Cowgirl Kate and Cocoa* by Erica Silverman, Harcourt, 2006 (Lesson 10)
- *Pepper's Journal: A Kitten's First Year* by Stuart Murphy, HarperCollins, 2000 (Lesson 12)
- *Purple, Green, and Yellow* by Robert Munsch, Annikins, 2007 (Lesson 13)
- *How Is a Crayon Made?* by Oz Charles, Aladdin, 1990 (Lesson 13)
- *Too Much Noise* by Ann McGovern, Sandpiper, 1992 (Lesson 14)
- *A Whisper Is Quiet* by Carolyn Lunn, Children's Press, 1988 (Lesson 14)
- *Noisy Neighbors* by Nicola Moon, Kingfisher, 2004 (Lesson 15)
- *It's Hard to Share My Teacher* by Joan Prestine, Fearon Teacher Aids, 1994 (Lesson 16)
- *Mine! Mine! Mine!* by Shelly Becker, Sterling, 2006 (Lesson 16)

Unit 3: Concepts of Print

- *Shiver Me Letters* by June Sobel, Sandpiper, 2009
  (Lesson 17)

- *Big Pig and Little Pig* by David McPhail, Green Light Readers, 2003
  (Lesson 18)

- *Big Dog...Little Dog* by P. D. Eastman, Random House, 2003
  (Lesson 18)

- *Big Al and Shrimpy* by Andrew Clements, Atheneum, 2005
  (Lesson 18)

- *Chicka Chicka Boom Boom* by Bill Martin, Jr., Beach Lane, 2009
  (Lesson 19)

- *Little Old Big Beard and Big Young Little Beard* by Remy Charlip, Marshall
  Cavendish 2006
  (Lesson 19)

- *Tops & Bottoms* by Janet Stevens, Hazar, 1997
  (Lesson 20)

- *Red Light, Green Light* by Anastasia Suen, Gulliver Books, 2005
  (Lesson 21)

- *Left or Right?* by Karl Rehm, Scholastic, 1993
  (Lesson 21)

- *The Alphabet Keeper* by Mary Murphy, Knopf, 2003
  (Lesson 22)

- *Mouse Makes Words* by Kathryn Heling, Random House, 2002
  (Lesson 22)

Unit 4: Labeling

- *Eating the Alphabet* by Lois Ehlert, Harcourt, 1996
  (Lessons 23 and 24)

- *Feathers for Lunch* by Lois Ehlert, Voyager Books, 1996
  (Lessons 23 and 24)

- *Cassie's Word Quilt* by Faith Ringgold, Dragonfly Books, 2004
  (Lessons 23 and 24)

- *Of Colors and Things* by Tana Hoban, Greenwillow, 1996
  (Lessons 23 and 24)

- *Richard Scarry's Best Word Book Ever* by Richard Scarry, Golden Books, 1980
  (Lesson 25)

- *Scholastic Children's Dictionary*, Scholastic, 2007
  (Lesson 25)

Unit 5: Mechanics of the Writing Process

- *Alphabet Mystery* by Audrey Wood, Blue Sky Press, 2003
  (Lesson 29)

Unit 6: Tools to Help Us Write

- *If You Give a Mouse a Cookie* by Laura Numeroff, Scholastic, 1985
  (Lesson 33)

- *Too Many Frogs* by Sandy Asher, Philomel, 2005
  (Lesson 34)

- *A Crowded Ride in the Countryside* by Frank B. Edwards, Pokeweed Press, 2002
  (Lesson 34)

- *The Boy Who Loved Words* by Ron Schotter, Schwartz and Wade, 2006
  (Lesson 36)

- *Max's Words* by Byron Barton, Farrar, Straus, 2006
  (Lesson 36)

- *First Thousand Words in English* by Heather Amery, Usborn, 2003
  (Lesson 36)

- *Frida's Office Day* by Thomas P. Lewis, HarperCollins, 1989
  (Lesson 37)

- *Lyle at the Office* by Bernard Waber, Sandpiper, 1996
  (Lesson 37)

- *Bea and Mr. Jones* by Amy Schwartz, Harcourt, 2006
  (Lesson 37)

- *Chrysanthemum* by Kevin Henkes, Greenwillow Books, 2007
  (Lesson 39)

- *The Name Jar* by Yangsook Choi, Dragonfly Books, 2003
  (Lesson 39)

- *My Name Is Yoon* by Helen Recorvits, Farrar, Straus, 2003
  (Lesson 39)

- *A Porcupine Named Fluffy* by Helen Lester, Sandpiper, 1989
  (Lesson 39)

- *My Many Colored Days* by Dr. Seuss, Knopf, 1998
  (Lesson 40)

- *A Color of His Own* by Leo Lionni, Knopf, 2006
  (Lesson 40)

- *One Fish, Two Fish, Red Fish, Blue Fish* by Dr. Seuss, Random House, 1988
  (Lesson 41)

- *Ten Apples Up On Top* by Dr. Seuss, Random House, 1961
  (Lesson 41)

- *Anno's Counting Book* by Mitsumasa Anno, Harper Festival, 1992
  (Lesson 41)

- *Today Is Monday* by Eric Carle, Penguin, 2001
  (Lesson 42)

- *Noodle* by Munro Leaf, Arthur A. Levine, 2006
  (Lesson 43)

- *Arms and Legs and Other Limbs* by Allan Fowler, Children's Press, 1999
  (Lesson 44)

Unit 7: Telling Stories

- *Tell Me a Story, Mama* by Angela Johnson, Scholastic, 1989
  (Lesson 45)

- *If You Were a Writer* by Joan Lowery Nixon, Aladdin, 1995
  (Lesson 45)

- *Cherries and Cherry Pits* by Vera Williams, Greenwillow, 1991
  (Lesson 45)

- *The Treasure* by Uri Shulevitz, Farrar, Straus, 1978
  (Lesson 46)

- *Arthur Writes a Story* by Marc Brown, Little, Brown, 1998
  (Lesson 48)

- *The Stories Julian Tells* by Ann Cameron, Random House, 1989
  (Lesson 50)

- Assorted wordless books by Mercer Mayer, Rain Bird, 2004
  (Lesson 51)

- *Ish* by Peter H. Reynolds, Candlewich, 2004
  (Lesson 52)

- *Corduroy* by Don Freeman, Puffin, 1990
  (Lesson 53)

Unit 8: Using Punctuation

- *Miss Mary Mack* by Mary Ann Hoberman, Little, Brown, 2003
  (Lesson 54)

- *The Napping House* by Joy Cowley, Harcourt, 1991
  (Lesson 54)

- *Pumpkin Pumpkin* by Jeanne Titherington, Greenwillow, 1990
  (Lesson 54)

- *Is Your Mama a Llama?* by Deborah Guarino, Scholastic, 2004
  (Lesson 55)

- *The Little Mouse, the Red Strawberry, and the Big Hungry Bear* by Don Wood
  and Audrey Wood, Child's Play International, 1984
  (Lesson 55)

- *No, David!* by David Shannon, Blue Sky, 1998
  (Lesson 56)

- *I Like Me!* by Nancy Carlson, Puffin, 1990
  (Lesson 56)

- *Today Is Monday* by Eric Carle, Putnam, 1997
  (Lesson 56)

- *Punctuation Pals* by Dr. Hope, Alpine Publishing, 2000
  (Lesson 57)

- *Perfect Pop-Up Punctuation Book* by Kate Petty, Dutton Juvenile, 2006
  (Lesson 57)

- *Punctuation Takes a Vacation* by Robin Pulver, Holiday House, 2004
  (Lesson 57)

Unit 9: Making Our Writing Even Better

- *Fix It, Sam* by Lori Ries, Charlesbridge, 2007
  (Lesson 58)

- *Fix-It Duck* by Jez Alborough, Picture Lions, 2002
  (Lesson 58)

Unit 10: Writing for Many Purposes

- *I Read Signs* by Tana Hoban, Harper Trophy, 1987
  (Lesson 66)

- *Signs at the Store* by Mary Hill, Children's Press, 2003
  (Lesson 66)

- *The Sign on Rosie's Door* by Maurice Sendak, HarperCollins, 2002
  (Lesson 66)

- *The List* by Hazel Hutchins, Annick Press, 2007
  (Lesson 67)

- *The 10 Best Things About My Dad* by Christine Loomis, Cartwheel, 2004
  (Lesson 67)

- *Wallace's Lists* by Barbara Bottner, Katherine Tegen Books, 2004
  (Lesson 67)

- *Sophie and the Mother's Day Card* by Kaye Umansky, Good Books, 1969
  (Lesson 68)

- *Happy Birthday, Good Knight* by Shelley Moore Thomas, Dutton Juvenile, 2006
  (Lesson 68)

- *The Jolly Postman* by Janet Ahlberg and Allan Ahlberg, LB Kids, 2006
  (Lesson 68)

- *A Letter to Amy* by Ezra Jack Keats, Puffin, 1998
  (Lesson 69)

- *Click, Clack, Moo: Cows That Type* by Doreen Cronin, Simon & Schuster, 2000
  (Lesson 69)

- *Dear Mr. Blueberry* by Simon James, Aladdin, 1996
  (Lesson 69)

- *Coyote School News* by Joan Sandin, Henry Holt, 2003
  (Lesson 70)

- *The Random House Book of Poetry For Children* by Jack Prelutsky, Random House, 1983
  (Lesson 71)

- *Poetry for Young People* by Langston Hughes, Sterling, 2006
  (Lesson 71)

- *Here's a Little Poem* by Jane Yolen, Candlewich, 2007
  (Lesson 71)

- *My Prairie Summer* by Sarah Glasscock, Raintree Steck-Vaughn, 2000
  (Lesson 72)

- *Diary of a Wombat* by Jackie French, Sandpiper, 2009
  (Lesson 72)
- *Diary of a Worm* by Doreen Cronin, HarperCollins, 2003
  (Lesson 72)
- *Owl Moon* by Jane Yolen, Philomel, 1987
  (Lesson 73)
- *The Paperboy* by Dav Pilkey, Scholastic, 1999
  (Lesson 73)
- *A Chair for My Mother* by Vera B. Williams, Greenwillow, 1984
  (Lesson 73)
- *Frogs* by Gail Gibbons, Scholastic, 1993
  (Lessons 74 and 75)
- *Dinosaurs* by Gail Gibbons, Scholastic, 1987
  (Lessons 74 and 75)
- *Monarch Butterfly* by Gail Gibbons, Scholastic, 1989
  (Lessons 74 and 75)

Fix It Up! Checklist

✔	Check My Writing
	1. ⟶ cat Do your pictures and words match?
	2. <u>A</u> cat is a pet. Does every sentence begin with an uppercase letter?
	3. X Have I X-ed out words that need to be fixed?
	4. ∧ Have I added any words that are missing?
	5. . ? ! Do all of my sentences end with a punctuation mark?

A Plan for Writing

1. Say your sentence out loud.

I like to play outside.

2. Put up one finger for each word.

3. Count the fingers that are up.

1 2 3 4 5

4. Say the sentence again, matching the words to your fingers.

I like to play outside.

5. Say the words one at a time and write them.

 I like to play outside

6. Reread your sentence.

 I like to play outside.

7. Stop your sentence with punctuation.

. ? !

Alphabet Chart

Aa	Bb	Cc	Dd	Ee	Ff
Gg	Hh	Ii	Jj	Kk	Ll
Mm	Nn	Oo	Pp	Qq	Rr
Ss	Tt	Uu	Vv	Ww	Xx
Yy	Zz				